PROGRAMMING IN C

PROGRAMMING IN C

By

P. Rizwan Ahmed

MCA, M.Sc., M.A., M.Phil,(Ph.D)

Head of the Department

Department of Information System Management

Mazharul Uloom College, Ambur, Vellore

Tamil Nadu

UNIVERSITY SCIENCE PRESS

(An Imprint of Laxmi Publications Pvt. Ltd.)

BANGALORE • CHENNAI • COCHIN • GUWAHATI • HYDERABAD
JALANDHAR • KOLKATA • LUCKNOW • MUMBAI • RANCHI
NEW DELHI • BOSTON, USA

Published by :

UNIVERSITY SCIENCE PRESS

(An Imprint of Laxmi Publications Pvt. Ltd.)

113, Golden House, Darya Ganj,
New Delhi-110 002

Phone : 011-43 53 25 00
Fax : 011-43 53 25 28

www.laxmipublications.com
info@laxmipublications.com

First Edition : 2014

OFFICES

© **Bangalore**	080-26 75 69 30	© **Chennai**	044-24 34 47 26
© **Cochin**	0484-237 70 04, 405 13 03	© **Guwahati**	0361-251 38 81
© **Hyderabad**	040-24 65 23 33	© **Jalandhar**	0181-222 12 72
© **Kolkata**	033-22 27 43 84	© **Lucknow**	0522-220 99 16
© **Mumbai**	022-24 91 54 15	© **Ranchi**	0651-220 44 64

UPC-9710-125-PROGRAMMING IN C-AHM C—

Typeset at : Sukuvisa Enterprises, New Delhi. *Printed at* : Repro Knowledgecast Limited, Thane

Dedicated to

My Parents

Mr Rasheed Ahmed

Mrs Farida Rasheed

and

My Wife

Mrs Sumira Rizwan

Preface

This book was developed specifically for freshmen students taking up their first course in programming, but people who are interested in learning C are also welcome to study it. Its aim is to supplement classroom lectures by focusing on C programming. Topics are arranged based on the order of class discussion.

I tried my level best to maintain a very simple language throughout the book to enable the readers to understand the concepts very easily.

May you learn a lot from the study of this book, and may the knowledge that you have gained be used for the common good of all people.

This book is written for the first course on Programming in C. It is very useful to B.Sc. Computer Science, B.Sc., Software Engineering, B.Sc. Information System Management, B.Sc. Software Computer Science, B.Sc. Electronics, B.Sc. Mathematics, B.Com Computer Applications, BCA, M.Sc. Information Technology, MCA, MBA, B.E./B.Tech and AMIE students. Review questions are added at the end of each chapter for practice purpose. This book contains the five chapters are summarized here:

Chapter 1 covers the Fundamentals of C Programming, Programming Elements, Operators, Expressions, Evaluation of Expressions and Library Functions. Chapter 2 contains Input and Output Statements, Decision-making Statements, and Looping Statements. Chapter 3 contains the functions, categories of functions, various storage classes, and recursion. Chapter 4 covers the Arrays, Structure and Union. Chapter 5 covers the pointers, operations on pointers, files and operation on files.

—Author

Acknowledgments

With its blessings of almighty it gives me a great pleasure to acknowledge our revered President of Ambur Muslim Educational Society (AMES) AliJanab Alhaj N. Md. Zackriah Sahib, General Secretary, Ali Janab Alhaj Nathersa Md Sayeed Sahib, Correspondent and Secretary Alijanab Alhaj Madekar Nazar Mohammed Sahib, Former Principal, Dr. D. Nisar Ahmed, Principal, Dr. P. M. Aadil Ahmed, M.Com, M.Phil., Ph.D, for their inspiration and encouragement in bringing out this book successfully.

I acknowledge our respected Prof. S. Joseph Gabriel, MCA, M.Phil., Associate Professor and Head of Computer Science and Prof. M. Mohammed Ismail, M.Sc.(IT)., M.Sc.(Phy.), M.Phil., PGDCA, Associate Professor in Computer Science and Chairman, Board of Studies in Computer Science and Computer Applications, Member, Academic Council, Thiruvalluvar University, Serkadu, Vellore, Prof. A. Herani Sahib, M.Sc., M.Phil., Associate Professor and Head of Mathematics, Chairman, Board of Examiners in Mathematics, Thiruvalluvar University, Vellore and Prof. A. Zakiuddin Ahmed, M.Sc., M.Phil., M.S, PGDCSM, Associate Professor in Computer Science, and Mr. A. Aqueel Ahmed, B.Sc., B.A., B.Ed., Mazharul Uloom College, Ambur for their constant support in bringing out this book.

I also thank my sister Shariha Sahifa and brother Mohammed Ramil, V.I Arshad Azeez for their patience and support extended to me all the times.

—Author

Contents

CHAPTER 1

FUNDAMENTALS OF C PROGRAMMING

1.1 HISTORY IN C

Introduction

C is a general-purpose computer programming language developed in 1972 by Dennis Ritchie at the Bell Telephone Laboratories for use with the Unix operating system. C is a structured programming language, which means that it allows you to develop programs using well-defined control structures (you will learn about control structures in the articles to come), and provides modularity (breaking the task into multiple sub tasks that are simple enough to understand and to reuse). C is often called a middle-level language because it combines the best elements of low-level or machine language with high-level languages.

1.2 WHY USE C?

C (and its object oriented version, C++) is one of the most widely used third generation programming languages. Its power and flexibility ensure it is still the leading choice for almost all areas of application, especially in the software development environment.

Many applications are written in C or C++, including the compilers for other programming languages. It is the language many operating systems are written in including UNIX, DOS and Windows. It continues to adapt to new uses, the latest being Java, which is used for programming Internet applications.

C has much strength, it is flexible and portable, it can produce fast, compact code, it provides the programmer with objects to create and manipulate complex structures (e.g. classes in C++) and low level routines to control hardware (e.g. input and output ports and operating system interrupts).

1.3 WHY LEARN C?

- Compact, fast, and powerful
- "Mid-level" Language

- Standard for program development (wide acceptance)
- It is everywhere! (Portable)
- Supports modular programming style
- Useful for all applications
- C is the native language of UNIX
- Easy to interface with system devices/assembly routines.

1.4 FEATURES OF C LANGUAGE

- It is a flexible high-level structured programming language.
- It includes the features of low-level language like assembly language.
- It is portable. A program written for one type of computer can be used in any other type.
- It is much ability and efficient.
- It has an ability to extend itself.
- It has a number of built-in functions, which makes the programming
- C is modular, as it supports functions to divide the program in to sub-program.
- C is efficient on most machines, because certain constructs are machine dependant.
- C language is well suited for structured programing, thus requiring the user to think of a problem in terms of function modules or blocks.

1.5 PROGRAMMING ELEMENTS

1.5.1 Character Set

Characters are used in a language to form words, numbers and expression. Characters used in C language can be grouped in to four types:

- Letters
- Digits
- Special Characters
- White Spaces

C Character Set	
Letters	**Digits**
Uppercase A – Z Lowercase a – z	0 to 9
Special characters	
, comma	+ plus
; semicolon	- minus
? question mark	< less than
$ dollar symbol	> greater than
# number sign	! exclamation mark
~ tild	% percentage
* asterisk	

White Spaces
Blank Space
Horizontal Tab
Carriage Return
New Line
Form Feed

1.5.2 Keywords

Keywords also referred as reserved words. Keywords have standard predefined specific meaning. The user has no right to change its meaning. Keywords should be written in lower case. They should be written in lower-case letters. The following keywords are reserved for C:

C Keywords			
Switch	Boolean	Break	Auto
For	Case	Const	Register
Char	Sizeof	Void	Static
Default	Do	Double	Struct
While	Continue	Float	Union
Include	Else	Go to	Short
Nested	For	Char	Signed
Int	If	Long	Volatile

1.5.3 Identifiers

Identifiers refer to the names of variables, functions and arrays. These are user-defined names and consist of a sequence of letters and digits with the letter as a first character. Both uppercase and lowercase letters are permitted although lowercase letters are commonly used. The underscore is used as a link between two words in long identifiers.

Rules for naming an identifiers

- Identifiers are formed with alphabets, digits and a special character underscore (_).
- The first character must be an alphabet.
- No special characters are allowed other than underscore.
- They are case sensitive. That it Sum is different from SUM.

For Example

Valid Identifiers	Invalid Identifiers
ROLL25	25ROLL
Register_No	Register No
CT100	100CT

1.5.4 Constants

A constant is a quantity whose value does not change during the execution of the program. There are three types of constants in C. They are:

1. Numeric Constants
2. Character Constants
3. String Constants

1. Numeric Constants

A numeric constants is a constants made up of digits and some special characters. There are two types of numeric constants. They are:

1. Integer or fixed point constants
2. Real or floating point constants

1. **Integer or Fixed Point Constants:** Integer constant is a constant made up of digits without decimal point. This can have values form –32, 768 to +32,767.

   For Example 125

2. **Real or Floating Point Constants:** Any number written with one decimal point is called real constant.

   For Example 98.50

2. Character Constants

Character constants are used to represent a alphabet within single quotes.

For Example 'F' 'G'

3. String Constants

String constants is a set of characters are represented with double quotes

For Example: "College" "school".

1.5.5 Data Types

Data types are used to store various types of data that is processed by program. Data type attaches with variable to determine the number of bytes to be allocate to variable and valid operations which can be performed on that variable. C supports various data types such as character, integer and floating-point types.

Data Type	Variable Type	Size	Range
Char	Character	1 byte or 8 bits	-128 to 127
Int	Integer	2 bytes	-32,768 to 32,767
Short	Short integer	1 byte	-32,768 to 32,767
Short int	Short integer	I byte	-32,768 to 32,767
Long	Long integer	4 bytes	-2,147,483,648 to 2,147,483,648
Unsigned char	Unsigned character	1 byte	0 to 255
Unsigned int	Unsigned int	2 bytes	0 to 65,535
Unsigned short	Unsigned short integer		0 to 65,535

Unsigned long	Unsigned long integer	4 bytes	0 to 4,294,967,295
Float	Floating point (7 digits)	4 bytes	3.4e-38 to 3.4e+38
Double	Floating point (15 digits)	8 bytes	1.7e-308 to 1.7e+308

1.6 VARIABLES

Variable is a quantity which changes during the execution of a program. Declaration does three things.

Variable is a name of memory location where we can store any data. It can store only single data (Latest data) at a time. In C, a variable must be declared before it can be used. Variables can be declared at the start of any block of code, but most are found at the start of each function.

1. It gives name to memory location.
2. It specifies the type of data.
3. It allocates memory space.

1.6.1 Rules for Naming Variables

- The first character in a variable name must be an alphabets, underscore (_), dollar sign($).
- Commas or blanks spaces are not allowed within a variable name.
- Variable names are case sensitive. (i.e., regno is different from REGNO)
- Uppercase and lowercase letters are distinct.
- The Variable name should not be a keyword.
- Variable names cannot contain blanks; use underscore instead.

1.6.2 Declaration of Variable

A declaration begins with the type, followed by the name of one variable.

The general format is

```
data_type variable_name;
```

where

Variablename: Every variable has a name and a value. The name identifies the variable, the value stores data. There is a limitation on what these names can be. Every variable name in C must start with a letter; the rest of the name can consist of letters, numbers and underscore characters. C recognizes upper and lower case characters as being different. Finally, you cannot use any of C's keywords like main, while, switch etc as variable names.

To declare multiple variables

A declaration begins with the type, followed by the name of one or more variables.

The general form is:

```
datatype var1,1var2,…….varn;
```

where,

datatype – any valid datatype

var1,var2,....varn - name of the variables

Some valid variable declarations are as follows:

For Example

```
int     count;
float   x,y;
double p1;
byte    b;
char    c1,c2,c3;
```

1.6.3 Initialization of Variables/Assigning Values to Variables

C Variables may be initialized with a value when they are declared. Consider the following declaration,

The general format is:

```
datatype variable_name = value or expression;
```

Example 1

```
int      a=10;
char     c='M';
String   str="MAN;
```

Example 2

The following example illustrates the two methods for variable initialization:

```
#include <stdio.h>
main ()
{
        int sum=33;
        float money=44.12;
        char letter;
        double pressure;
        letter='E'; /* assign character value */
        pressure=2.01e-10; /*assign double value */
        printf("value of sum is %d\n",sum);
        printf("value of money is %f\n",money);
        printf("value of letter is %c\n",letter);
        printf("value of pressure is %e\n",pressure);
}
```

The output of the above program is as follows:

value of sum is 33

value of money is 44.119999

value of letter is E

value of pressure is 2.010000e-10

Local Variables

Local variables are declared within the body of a function, and can only be used within that function only.

Syntex:

```
void main( ){
int a,b,c;
}
void fun1()
{
int x,y,z;
}
```

Here a, b, c are the local variable of void main() function and it can't be used within fun1() Function. And x, y and z are local variable of fun1().

Global Variable

A global variable declaration looks normal, but is located outside any of the program's functions. This is usually done at the beginning of the program file, but after preprocessor directives. The variable is not declared again in the body of the functions which access it.

Syntax:

```
#include<stdio.h>
int a,b,c;
void main()
{


}
void fun1()
{
}
```

Here a, b, c are global variable and these variable can be accessed (used) within a whole program.

1.7 STRUCTURE OF C-PROGRAM

The general structure of C-Program is

Include section
Main function
{
Variable declarations;
Method definitions
{

```
        Statement1;
        ----------
        ----------

        Statement n;
    }
}
```

Include Section

In this section the header files must be included. This depends on the functions used in the program statements. The include files must begin with # symbols.

For Example

#include<stdio.h>, #include<math.h> etc.

Main Functions

This function must present in all programs. This gives the starting point of the program.

Variable Declaration

In this section the user has to declare the variables which are local to the main block.

Method Definition

This is an optional section. This section is used to write sub-programs.

Statements

In this section the user can write valid C statements to solve the problem.

1.8 OPERATORS

An operator is a symbol which helps the user to command the computer to do a certain mathematical or logical manipulations. Operators are used in C language program to operate on data and variables. C has a rich set of operators which can be classified as

1. Arithmetic Operators
2. Relational Operators
3. Logical Operators
4. Assignment Operators
5. Increment & Decrement Operators
6. Bitwise Operators
7. Conditional Operators
8. Special Operators

1.8.1 Arithmetic Operators

Arithmetic operators are used to perform arithmetic calculations. C provides basic arithmetic operators. They are +,-,*, /, %

Table shows you, the different Arithmetic operators that were used in C programming.

Table: Arithmetic Operators

Operators	Example	Meaning
+	a+b	Addition (or) Unary plus
-	a-b	Subtraction (or) Unary minus
*	a*b	Multiplication
/	a/b	Division
%	a%b	Modulo division (Remainder)

Example

```
/** program using Arithmetic operators **/
#include<stdio.h>
main()
{
        int a,b,c;
        printf("enter the a and b values:" );
        scanf("%d%D",&a,&b);
        c=a+b;
        printf(" C value is%d ", c);
}
```

1.8.2 Relational Operators

Relational operators are used to find out the relationship between two operands. Table shows you the different relational operators used in C programming.

Operator	Operations	Example
<	Less than	a<b
>	Greater than	a>b
<=	Less than or equal to	a<=b
>=	Greater than equal to	a>=b
==	Equal to	a==b
!=	Not equal to	a!=b

Example

```
#include<stdio.h>
int main(void)
{
        int n1,n2;
```

```
        printf("enter the two numbers");
        scanf("%d%d",&n1,&n2);
        if(n1==n2)
        {
                printf("%d is equal to %d\n",n1,n2);
        }
        if(n1!=n2)
        {
                printf("%d is not equal to %d\n",n1,n2);
        }
        if(n1<n2)
        {
                printf("%d is less than  %d\n",n1,n2);
        }
        if(n1<=n2)
        {
                printf("%d is less than or equal to %d\n",n1,n2);
        }
        if(n1>=n2)
        {
                printf("%d is greater than or equal to %d\n",n1,n2);
        }
        retrun 0;
    }
}
```

1.8.3 Logical Operators

Logical operator is used to find out the relationship between two or more relationship expressions. Table 2.3 shows you the different logical operators used in C Programming.

Operators	Meaning
&&	Logical AND
| |	Logical OR
!	Logical NOT

The logical operators && and | | are used when we want to form compound conditions by combining two or more relations.

Logical operators return results indicated in the following table.

X	Y	x && y	x || y
T	T	T	T
T	F	F	T
F	T	F	T
F	T	F	F

Logical AND (&&)

This operator is used to evaluate 2 conditions or expressions with relational operators simultaneously. If both the expressions to the left and to the right of the logical operator is true then the whole compound expression is true.

Example

a > b && x = = 10

The expression to the left is a > b and that on the right is x == 10 the whole expression is true only if both expressions are true i.e., if a is greater than b and x is equal to 10.

Logical OR (||)

The logical OR is used to combine 2 expressions or the condition evaluates to true if any one of the 2 expressions is true.

Example a < m || a < n

The expression evaluates to true if any one of them is true or if both of them are true. It evaluates to true if a is less than either m or n and when a is less than both m and n.

Logical NOT (!)

The logical not operator takes single expression and evaluates to true if the expression is false and evaluates to false if the expression is true. In other words it just reverses the value of the expression.

For example

! (x >= y) the NOT expression evaluates to true only if the value of x is neither greater than or equal to y.

1.8.4 Assignment Operators

Assignment operators are used to assign the value of an expression to a variable. The Assignment Operator evaluates an expression on the right of the expression and substitutes it to the value or variable on the left of the expression. The general form is

```
V op=exp;
```

Where,

V - variable

Exp - expression

Op - C binary operators

= - Is known as the assignment operators.

V op=exp; is equal to V=V op (exp);

i.e.,

x+=y+1; is equal to x=x+(y+1);

The table given below lists the assignment operators with example operator descriptions.

Table: Assignment Operators

Operators	Meaning	Expression	
+=	Add assign	X+=a	X=x+a
-=	Sub assign	X - = a X=x-a	X=x-a
*=	Multiple assign	X*=a	X=x*a
/	Division	X/=a	X=x/a
%	Modulo	X%=a	X=x%a

Example

x = a + b

Here the value of a + b is evaluated and substituted to the variable x.

In addition, C has a set of shorthand assignment operators of the form.

1.8.5 Increment and Decrement Operators

C has two very useful operators. They are increment (++) and decrement (--) operators. The increment operator (++) add 1 to the operator value contained in the variable. The decrement operator (--) subtract from the value contained in the variable. The increment and decrement operators are one of the unary operators which are very useful in C language. They are extensively used in for and while loops.

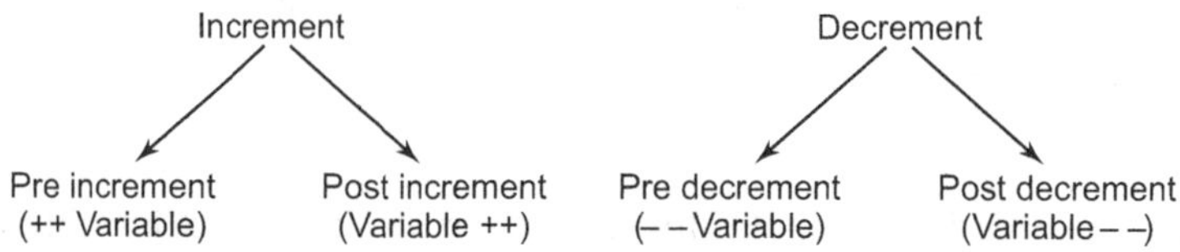

The increment operator ++ adds the value 1 to the current value of operand and the decrement operator – – subtracts the value 1 from the current value of operand. ++variable name and variable name++ mean the same thing when they form statements independently, they behave differently when they are used in expression on the right hand side of an assignment statement.

Example

Consider the following:

m = 5;

y = ++m; (prefix)

In this case the value of y and m would be 6

Suppose if we rewrite the above statement as

m = 5;

y = m++; (post fix)

Then the value of y will be 5 and that of m will be 6. A prefix operator first adds 1 to the operand and then the result is assigned to the variable on the left. On the other hand, a postfix operator first assigns the value to the variable on the left and then increments the operand.

1.8.6 Bitwise Operators

Bitwise operators are used to perform bit by bit operations. A bitwise operator operates on each bit of data. Those operators are used for testing, complementing or shifting bits to the right on left. Bitwise operators may not be applied to a float or double. The table given below lists the various bitwise operators.

Table: Bitwise Operators

Operators	Meaning
&	Bitwise AND
|	Bitwise OR
^	Bitwise Exclusive OR
>>	Bitwise Right Shift
<<	Bitwise Left Shift
~	Bitwise Complement

Bitwise AND (&)

The bitwise operations are carried out between two bit patterns.

Example

Let x=0101 y= 1011

x & y =0001

Bitwise OR(| |)

The bitwise operations is carried out between two bit patterns.

Let x=0100 y=1011

x | y = 1111

Bitwise exclusive OR(^)

Let x=0010 y=1010

x ^ y = 1000

1.8.7 Conditional Operator

The conditional operators are also called ternary operator. It is used to construct conditional expressions. Conditional operator has three operands. The general format is:

```
condition?expression1:expression2;
```

If the result of **condition** is TRUE (non-zero), **expression1** is evaluated and the result of the evaluation becomes the result of the operation. If the condition is FALSE (zero), then **expression2** is evaluated and its result becomes the result of the operation.

For Example

```
int x=10, y=15;
int y= (x>y)?x : y;
```

In the above example, check x>10, if is true, print x value otherwise y.

1.8.8 Special Operators

C supports some special operators of interest such as comma operator, size of operator, pointer operators (& and *) and member selection operators (. and ->). The size of and the comma operators are discussed here. The remaining operators are discussed in forth coming chapters.

1.8.8.1 The Comma Operator

The comma operator can be used to link related expressions together. A comma-linked list of expressions are evaluated left to right and value of right most expression is the value of the combined expression.

Example

value = (x = 10, y = 5, x + y);

First assigns 10 to x and 5 to y and finally assigns 15 to value. Since comma has the lowest precedence in operators the parenthesis is necessary. Some examples of comma operator are

In for loops:

for (n=1, m=10, n <=m; n++,m++)

In while loops

While (c=getchar(), c != '10')

Exchanging values.

t = x, x = y, y = t;

1.8.8.2 The Size of Operator

The operator size of gives the size of the data type or variable in terms of bytes occupied in the memory. The operand may be a variable, a constant or a data type qualifier.

Example

m = sizeof (sum);

n = sizeof (long int);

k = sizeof (235L);

The size of operator is normally used to determine the lengths of arrays and structures when their sizes are not known to the programmer. It is also used to allocate memory space dynamically to variables during the execution of the program.

1.9 OPERATOR PRECEDENCE AND ASSOCIATIVITY

Table: Precedence and Associativity of Operators

`() [] ->`	Left to right
`! ~ ++ -- + - *` *(type)* `sizeof`	Right to left

* / %	left to right
+ -	left to right
<< >>	left to right
< <= > >=	left to right
== !=	left to right
&	left to right
^	left to right
|	left to right
&&	left to right
||	left to right
?:	right to left
= += -= *= /= %= &= ^= |= <<= >>=	tight to left

Example

Write a C program to print the message "Welcome to C Program."

```
#include< stdio.h>
int main()
{
   printf("Welcome to C program");
}
```

- The C program starting point is identified by the word main().
- This informs the computer as to where the program actually starts. The parentheses that follow the keyword main indicate that there are no arguments supplied to this program.
- The two braces, { and }, signify the begin and end segments of the program. In general, braces are used throughout C to enclose a block of statements to be treated as a unit.
- The purpose of the statement #include <stdio.h> is to allow the use of the printf statement to provide program output. For each function built into the language, an associated header file must be included. Text to be displayed by printf() must be enclosed in double quotes. The program only has the one printf() statement.
- printf( ) is actually a function (procedure) in C that is used for printing variables and text. Where text appears in double quotes "", it is printed without modification. There are some exceptions however. This has to do with the \ and % characters. These characters are modifiers, and for the present the \ followed by the n character represents a newline character.

1.10 CREATION AND EXECUTION OF A C-PROGRAM

The following steps are followed for creating and executing a C-Program.

Step-1: Creating or Editing the C- Program

Using any editor, we can create the program with C extension. Usually we use TC or Turbo editor. For Example: Sample.C

Step-2: Compiling and Executing a C Program

Using Alt+F9 keys in TC editor, the program can be compiled and linked. This produces the executable program with .exe extension. For Example: Sample.exe

Using Ctrl+F9 we can run the .exe program and produce the required result.

Sample C Program

Write a C Program to Computer Simple and Compound Interest.

```
#include<stdio.h>
#include<math.h>
Main( )
{
      Float p,n,r,simple,compound;
      Printf("Enter principle amount");
      Scanf("%f", &p);
      Printf("Enter the rate of interest");
      Scanf("%f", &r);
      Printf("Enter the time period in years");
      Scanf("%f", &n);
      Simple=p*n*r/100;
      Compound=p*pow(1+r/100,t)-p;
      Printf("simple interest is \n &6.2f",
                              simple);
      printf("\n");
      printf("compound interest is \n\n%6.2f",
                                   compound);
}
```

1.11 EXPRESSIONS

An expression is a linear combination of constants, variables and operators. There are three types of expressions. They are:

1. Arithmetic Expressions
2. Relational Expressions
3. Logical Expressions

1. **Arithmetic Expressions:** Arithmetic Expressions are formed by connecting constants of variables by arithmetic operators. The general form is:

   `variable Arithmetic operator variable`

Example

```
x+y+z
(x+y)/z
(x+y)/(z/a)
```

2. **Relational Expressions:** Relational Expressions are formed by connecting constants or variable or arithmetic expressions by relational operators. The general form is

   `variable relational operator variable`

Example

```
a==10
a>=b
```

3. **Logical Expressions:** Logical expressions are formed by connecting relational expressions by logical operators. The general format is

```
Variable logical operator variable
```

Example

```
a>10 && b>20
salary>5000 && DA>=500
```

1.12 EVALUATION OF EXPRESSIONS

In "C" expressions are evaluated by assignment statement.

```
Variable = expression
```

Example

```
X=a+b/c;
Z=(x/y)+(a/b)
```

1.12.1 Precedence of Arithmetic Operators

Highest operator	- * / %
Lowest operator	- +, -

Example

Consider the expression given below:

5+8(3+1)+12*4+3

Step1 – 5+8/4+12*4+3

Step2 - 5+2+12*4+3

Step3 – 5+2+48+3

Step4 – 58

Example

```
#include<stdio.h>
main()
{
        float a,b,c,x,y,z;
        a=9;
        b=12;
        c=3;
        x=a-b/3+c*2-1;
        y=a-b/(3+c)*(2-1);
        z=a-(b/(3+c)*2)-1;
        printf("x=%d", x);
        printf("y=%d", y);
        printf("z=%d", z);
}
```

1.13 LIBRARY FUNCTIONS

Library Functions are functions not to be written by the programmer. But these are available in separate files called header files. The commonly used predefined functions are as follows:

(*i*) string function(string.h) or string handling functions.

(*ii*) math function(math.h)

1.13.1 String Functions (string.h) or String Handling Functions

String are the combination of number of characters these are used to store any word in any variable of constant. A string is an array of character. It is internally represented in system by using ASCII value. Every single character can have its own ASCII value in the system. A character string is stored in one array of character type.

e.g. "Ram" contains ASCII value per location, when we are using strings and then these strings are always terminated by character '\0'. We use conversion specifies %s to set any string we can have any string as follows:-

char nm [25].

When we store any value in nm variable then it can hold only 24 character because at the end of the string one character is consumed automatically by '\0'.

The important string functions are given below:

(*i*) strlen()

(*ii*) strcpy()

(*iii*) strcat()

(*iv*) strupr()

(*v*) strlwr()

strlen()

This function is sued to find out the number of characters in the given string. The general format is

```
n=strlen(string);
```

where,

n - length of the string.

String - valid string variable

Example

```
N=strlen("mucollege")
```

Output: 9

strcpy()

This function is used to copy the content of one string to another string. The general form is

```
strcpy(string1, string2);
```

Where,

String1& string - valid string variable

Example

```
String2="mucollege";
Strcpy(string1,string2);
```

Output

String1= mucollege

strcat()

This function is used to concatenate (merge or join) two strings. The general form is

```
strcat(string1, string2);
```

Where,

String1 & string2 - valid string variable

Example

```
String1 = "engineering";
String2=" college";
Strcat(string1,string2);
```

Output

String1= engineering college
String2=college

strupr()

`strupr( )` function is used to convert a string in lowercase to uppercase. The general format is

```
N=strupr(string);
```

Example

```
N=Strupr("muc");
```

Output: MUC

strlwr()

`strlwr( )` function is used to convert a string in uppercase to lowercase. The general format is

```
N=strlwr(string);
```

Example

```
String="MUCOLLEGE";
N=strlwr(string);
```

Output:

Mucollege

Example Program

//program to demonstrate string handling functions

```
#include <stdio.h>
#include <conio.h>
int main()
{
```

```
    char a[50];
    char b[50];
    printf("Please the two strings one by one\n");
    gets(a);
    gets(b);
    printf("Length of String a is %d \n",strlen(a));
    printf("Length of String b is %d \n",strlen(b));
 if(!strcmp(a,b))
    printf("Both the strings are Equal");
 else
    printf("Both the strings are not equal");
    strcat(a,b); //Concatenation function
    printf("the concatenated String is:");
    puts(a);
    strrev(a);
    printf("The reverse string is\n");
    puts(a);
    getch();
    return 0;
 }
```

1.13.2 Math Function(math.h)

The important math functions are given below:

1. sin()
2. cos()
3. tan()
4. exp()
5. ceil()
6. floor()
7. abs()

1. sin()

   `sin()` function is used to find the sine value of the given argument. The general format is

   `Sin(double x);`

2. cos()

   `cos()` function is used to cosine the value of the given argument. The general format is

   `Cos( double x);`

3. tan()

   `tan()` function is used to tangent value of the given argument. The general format is

   `Tan(double x);`

4. exp()

   `exp()` function is used return exponential value of the given argument. The general format is

   `Exp(double x);`

5. ceil()

   `ceil()` function is used to round the given argument(real number). The general format is

   ```
   Ceil(double x);
   ```

6. floor()

   `floor()` function is used to round the given argument(real number). The general format is

   ```
   Floor(double x)
   ```

7. abs()

   `abs()` function is used to find the absolute value of an integer. The general format is

   ```
   abs(int x);
   ```

8. sqrt()

   Sqrt() function is used to find the square root value of a given number. The general format is

   Sqrt(int x)

1.14 THE C PREPROCESSOR

The C preprocessor is a tool which filters your source code before it is compiled. The preprocessor allows constants to be named using the #define notation. The preprocessor provides several other facilities which will be described here. It is particularly useful for selecting machine dependent pieces of code for different computer types, allowing a single program to be compiled and run on several different computers.

The C preprocessor isn't restricted to use with C programs, and programmers who use other languages may also find it useful, however it is tuned to recognize features of the C language like comments and strings, so its use may be restricted in other circumstances. The preprocessor is called cpp, however it is called automatically by the compiler so you will not need to call it while programming in C.

Using #define to Implement Constants

We have already met this facility, in its simplest form it allows us to define textual substitutions as follows:

```
#define MAXSIZE 256
```

This will lead to the value 256 being substituted for each occurrence of the word MAXSIZE in the file.

Using #define to Create Functional Macros

#define can also be given arguments which are used in its replacement. The definitions are then called macros. Macros work rather like functions, but with the following minor differences.

- Since macros are implemented as a textual substitution; there is no effect on program performance (as with functions).
- Recursive macros are generally not a good idea.
- Macros don't care about the type of their arguments. Hence macros are a good choice where we might want to operate on real, integers or a mixture of the two. Programmers sometimes call such type flexibility polymorphism.

- Macros are generally fairly small.

  Macros are full of traps for the unwary programmer. In particular the textual substitution means that arithmetic expressions are liable to be corrupted by the order of evaluation rules.

Reading in Other Files using #include

The preprocessor directive #include is an instruction to read in the entire contents of another file at that point. This is generally used to read in header files for library functions. Header files contain details of functions and types used within the library. They must be included before the program can make use of the library functions.

Library header file names are enclosed in angle brackets, < >. These tell the preprocessor to look for the header file in the standard location for library definitions. This is /usr/include for most UNIX systems.

For example

```
#include <stdio.h>
```

Another use for #include for the programmer is where multi-file programs are being written. Certain information is required at the beginning of each program file. This can be put into a file called globals.h and included in each program file. Local header file names are usually enclosed by double quotes, " ". It is conventional to give header files a name which ends in .h to distinguish them from other types of file.

Our globals.h file would be included by the following line.

```
#include "globals.h"
```

Conditional selection of code using #ifdef

The preprocessor has a conditional statement similar to C's if else. It can be used to selectively include statements in a program. This is often used where two different computer types implement a feature in different ways. It allows the programmer to produce a program which will run on either type.

The keywords for conditional selection are; #ifdef, #else and #endif.

#ifdef takes a name as an argument, and returns true if the name has a current definition. The name may be defined using a #define, the -d option of the compiler, or certain names which are automatically defined by the UNIX environment.

#else is optional and ends the block beginning with #ifdef. It is used to create a 2 way optional selection.

#endif ends the block started by #ifdef or #else.

Where the #ifdef is true, statements between it and a following #else or #endif are included in the program. Where it is false, and there is a following #else, statements between the #else and the following #endif are included.

This is best illustrated by an example.

Using #ifdef for Different Computer Types

Conditional selection is rarely performed using #defined values. A simple application using machine dependent values is illustrated below.

```
#include <stdio.h>
main()
{
#ifdef vax
printf("This is a VAX\n");
#endif
#ifdef sun
printf("This is a SUN\n");
#endif
}
```

Sun is defined automatically on SUN computers. vax is defined automatically on VAX computers.

Using #ifdef to temporarily remove program statements

#ifdef also provides a useful means of temporarily `blanking out' lines of a program. The lines in question are preceded by #ifdef NEVER and followed by #endif. Of course you should ensure that the name NEVER isn't defined anywhere.

LET US SUMMARISE

- C is an efficient and portable general purpose programming language.
- Algorithm is defined as a step by step procedure to solve a problem. It can be written in any language.
- A flow chart is a graphical representation of an algorithm is called flow chart.
- Characters are used in a language to form words, numbers and expression.
- A constant is a quantity whose value does not change during the execution of the program.
- Keywords also referred as reserved words.
- Data types are used to store various types of data that is processed by program.
- Variable is a quantity which changes during the execution of a program.

REVIEW QUESTIONS

1. What is Character set?
2. Define Identifiers.
3. List out any two rules for naming variables.
4. What are the various types of operators in C?
5. What are keywords?
6. Define Constants.
7. What is Expressions?
8. Define ternary operator.
9. Define Library Functions.
10. What is string?

EXERCISES

1. Write a C-program to find the sum and average of three real numbers.
2. Write a C-program to find area and perimeter of a circle.
3. Write a C-program to print the sample interest.
4. Write a C-program to convert centigrade to farenheit temperature.
5. Write a C-program to convert farenheit to centigrade temperature.

CHAPTER 2

I/O AND CONTROL STATEMENTS

2.1 I/O STATEMENTS

Reading, processing, and writing of data are the three essential functions of a computer program. Most programs take some data as input and display the processed data, often known as information or results, on a suitable medium. There are two methods of providing data to the program variables. One method is to assign values through the assignment statements such as x = 5; a = 0; and so on.

Another method is to use the input function **scanf** that can read data from a keyboard. We have used both the methods in most of our earlier example programs. For outputting results we have used extensively the function **printf**, which sends results out to a terminal. All input-output operations are carried out through function calls such as **printf** and **scanf**. There exist several functions that have more or less become standard for input and output operations in C. These functions are collectively known as the standard I/O library. The first statement of a C Program is

 # include < stdio. h >

This is to instruct the compiler to fetch the standard input/output function from the C library, and that it is not a part of C language. However, there might be exceptions. For example, this is not necessary for the functions **printf** and **scanf** which have been defined as a part of the C language. The file name **stdio.h** is an abbrevation for standard input-output header file. The instruction **#include <stdio.h>** tells the compiler 'to search for a file named **stdio.h** and place its contents at this point in the program. The contents of the header file become part of the source code when it is compiled # is a pre-processor.

2.1.1 Single Character I/O

Single Character Input : `getchar()`

The `getchar( )` function reads a single character from the keyboard. It takes no parameters and it's returned value is the input character. The general format is

```
Variable = getchar();
```

Example

```
Char c;
C=getchar();
```

`getchar()` reads a character from the keyboard and assigns it to c.

Single Character Output: `putchar()`

The putchar() function displays a single character on the screen. The general format is:

```
putchar(variable)
```

Example

```
putchar(c);
```

2.2 FORMATTED I/O

C provides two functions that gives formatted I/O : scanf( ) and printf( ).

2.2.1 Formatted Input: `scanf( )`

This function reads character, strings are well as numeric values from the standard input. The general format is:

```
scanf("format string", argument list);
```

The following table show what format specifiers should be used with what data types:

Code	Meaning
%c	read a single character
%d	read a decimal integer
%f	read a floating point value
%e	read a floating point value (even in exponential format)
%g	read a floating point value
%h	read a decimal, heaxadecimal or octal integer
%o	read an octal integer
%s	read a string
%u	read an unsigned integer
%x	read a hexadecimal integer

Example

```
scanf("%d", &x);
```

Here,

x is an integer value.

2.2.2 Formatted Output :`printf()`

The `printf ( )` function is used to display values or results at the terminal. This function can be used to output any combination of numerical values, single characters and strings.

```
printf(" control string", argument list);
```

Where the control string consists of 1) literal text to be displayed, 2) format specifiers, and 3) special characters. The arguments can be variables, constants, expressions, or function calls -- anything that produces a value which can be displayed. Number of arguments must match the number of format identifiers. Unpredictable results if argument type does not "match" the identifier.

The following table show what format specifiers should be used with what data types:

Code	Meaning
%c	character
%d	decimal integer
%o	octal integer (leading 0)
%x	hexadecimal integer (leading 0x)
%u	unsigned decimal integer
%ld	long int
%f	floating point
%lf	double or long double
%e	exponential floating point
%s	character string

Example

```
printf( " Welcome to c programming");
```

The above statement prints the output as `welcome to c programming`.

2.3 STRING I/O FUNCTIONS

2.3.1 String Input : `gets()`

The `gets ( )` function is used to read a string form the keyboard until a carriage return key is pressed.

```
gets(s)
```

Where s is the name of the array storing the string.

Example

```
char name[20];
gets(name);
```

2.3.2 String Output : `puts()`

The `puts( )` function outputs the string of characters stored in variable on the screen. The general format is

```
puts(s);
```

Where s is the name of the variable containing the text to be displayed.

Example

```
char name[20];
gets(name);
puts(name);
```

2.4 SAMPLE C PROGRAMS

Write a c program to print your rollno, name, address.

```
#include<stdio.h>
main()
{
        printf("Rollno\1001");
        printf("name="Faizan");
        printf("No.25, SK Road, Ambur");
}
```

Write a C program to add two numbers

```
#include<stdilo.h>
main()
{
        Int a,b,c;
        Printf("enter the two values a and b");
        Scanf("%d%d", &a,&b);
        C=a+b;
        Printf("C=%d", c);
}
```

Write a C program to subtract two numbers

```
#include<stdio.h>
main()
{
        int a,b,c;
        printf("enter the two values a and b");
        scanf("%d%d", &a,&b);
        c=a-b;
        printf("C=%d", c);
}
```

Write a C program to multiply two numbers

```
#include<stdio.h>
main()
{
        int a,b,c;
        printf("enter the two values a and b");
        scanf("%d%d", &a,&b);
        c=a*b;
        printf("C=%d", c);
}
```

Write a C program to divide two numbers

```
#include<stdio.h>
main()
{
        int a,b,c;
        printf("enter the two values a and b");
        scanf("%d%d", &a,&b);
        c=a/b;
        printf("C=%d", c);
}
```

Write a C program to add, subtract, multiply and divide two numbers

```
#include<stdio.h>
main()
{
        int a,b,add,sub,mul,div;
        printf("enter the two values a and b");
        scanf("%d%d", &a,&b);
        add=a+b;
        sub=a-b;
        mul=a*b;
        div=a/b;
        printf("add=%d", add);
        printf("sub=%d", sub);
        printf("mul=%d", mul);
        printf("div=%d", div);
}
```

2.5 CONTROL STATEMENTS/CONTROL FLOW/PROGRAMMING FLOW CONTROL

Control statements are used to transfer control from one statement to any other statement in a program. The control statements are classified as shown in the Fig. 2.1.

2.5.1 Decision–Making Statement

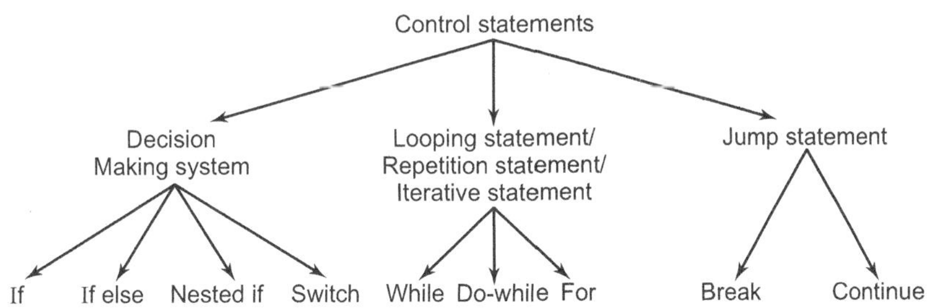

FIGURE 2.1

2.5.1.1 Simple if statement

Simple if statement is used to execute or skip on one statement or set of statements for a particular condition. The general format is

```
if(test condition)
{
        Statement block(s);
}
next statement;
```

If the test condition is true, statement block will be executed, otherwise execution starts from the next statement.

The following flow chart explains the working of the if statement:

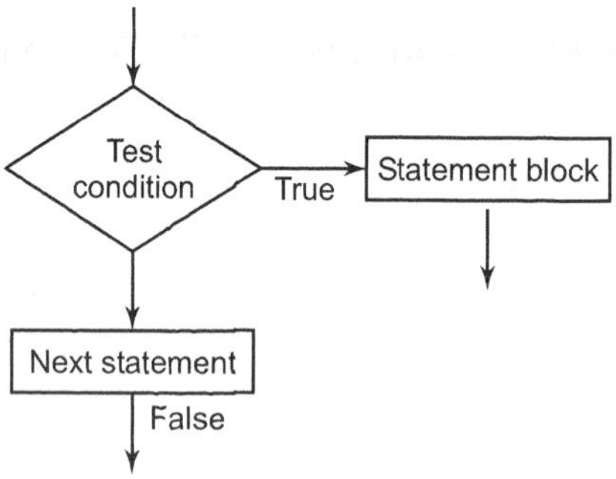

FIGURE 2.2

Example

Write a C program to demonstrate the use of if statement.

```
#include<stdio.h>
main()
{
    int mark;
    printf("Enter the marks");
    scanf("%d", &mark);
    if(mark>=70)
    {
        mark=mark+10;
        printf("Marks= %d", mark);
    }

}
```

Compile and execute the above program.

Enter the marks

75

The output of the above program is shown here

Mark=85

In the above example, test the mark of student. If the student mark is equal to 70 then 10 marks will be added to the mark statement.

2.5.1.2 if...else Statement

if...else Statement is used to execute one group of statements.

Syntax:-

```
if(test condition)
{
        True block Statement(s);
else
        False block Statement(s);
}
```

(*i*) If the test condition is true, then the True block statement is executed and the control statements are transferred to the next statement.

(*ii*) If the test condition is false, then false block statement is executed and the control statement is transferred to the next statement.

The following flow chart explains the working of the if-else statement:

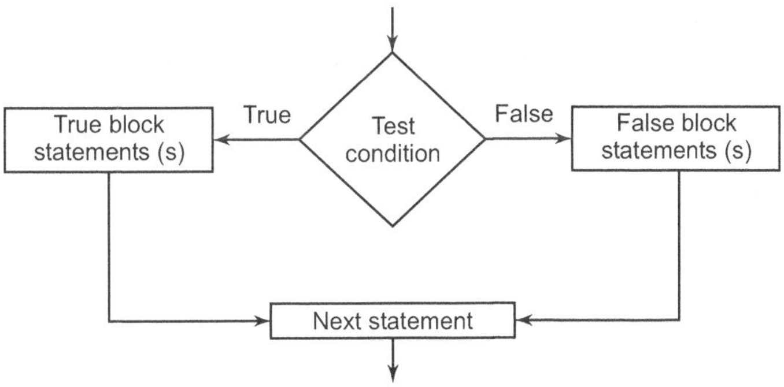

FIGURE 2.3

Example

Write a C program to find the biggest of two numbers.

```
#include<stdio.h>
main()
{
    int a,b;
    printf("Enter the a and b values");
    scanf("%d%d", &a,&b);
    if (a>b)
```

```
    {
            printf("A is bigger than b");
    }
    else
    {
            printf("b is bigger than a");
    }
}
```

Compile and execute the above program.

Enter the a and b values

10

5

The program displays the following output:

A is bigger than b

In the above example:

(*i*) This program test the true value of (a&b).

(*ii*) IF A is greater than B, it prints "A is bigger than B".

(*iii*) Otherwise, It prints "B is greater than A".

2.5.1.3 Nested-if Statement

If many decision makings occur in a program then, more than one if .. else can be used in nested if statement.

The general format is :

```
        if(test condition 1)
         {
         if(test condition 2)
         {
               Statement block 1;
         else
               Statement block 2;
         }
     else
               Statement block 3;
    }
    next Statement;
```

(*i*) The computer first evaluates the value of the test condition 1.

(*ii*) If test condition 1 is false, the control statement execute the statement block 3

(*iii*) If the test condition 1 is true, the control is transferred to test condition 2, if test condition 2 is true the statement block 1 is executed.

(*iv*) If the condition 2 is false statement block 2 is executed.

The following flow chart explains the working of the nested if statement:

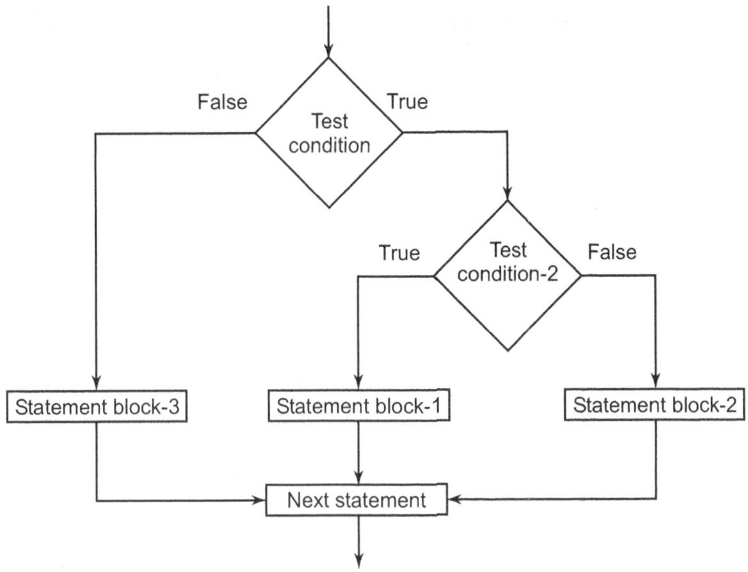

FIGURE 2.4

Example

Write a C program to find the biggest of three numbers.

```
#include<stdio.h>
main()
{
      int a, b, c;
      printf("enter  3 values");
      scanf("%d%d%d", &a,&b,&c);
      if (a>b)
      {
        if(b>c)
        {
           printf("B is bigger than C");
        }
      else
      {
         printf("C is bigger than B");
      }
```

```
else if(a>c)
{
  printf(A is bigger than C");
}
else
{
  printf("C is bigger than A");
}
}
}
```

Compile and execute the above program.

Enter 3 values:

10

15

5

The output of the above program is shown here:

B value 15 is large

Example 2

This program is to display the electricity bill calculation based on the number of units consumed every month

Input: The number of units – variable name – unit

Output: Amount of rupee – variable name – amount

Logic: Units	Rupees
1-50 units	0.75/unit
51-100	0.85/unit
101-200	1.50/unit
201-300	2.20/unit
>300	3.00/unit

```
#include <stdio.h>
#include <conio.h>
int main()
{
 float amount=0,units;
 printf("Enter the number of units");
 scanf("%f", &units);
if(units <=50)
```

```
{
   amount = units * 0.75;
}
else if(units >50 && units <=100)
{
   amount=0.75 * 50 + 0.85*(units-50);
}
else if(units >100 && units <200)
{
   amount=(0.75*50) + (0.85*50 )+ (1.5 *(units-100));
}
else if(units >200 && units <300)
{
amount=(0.75*50) + (0.85*50 )+ (1.5 *100) + (2.20*(units-200));
}
else
{
amount=(0.75*50) + (0.85*50 )+ (1.5 *100) + (2.20 * 100)
+(3.0*(units-300));
}
   amount=amount+(0.2*amount);
   printf("The total electricity bill is %f", amount);
   getch();
   return 0;
}
```

2.5.1.4 Switch Statement

The switch statement allows a number of choices. The general format of switch statement is shown here:

```
switch(expression)
{
      case  Label 1:
            Statement block 1;
            Break;
      case  Label 2:
            Statement block 2;
```

```
                Break;
                ---------------------
                ---------------------
          case  Label n:
                Statement block n;
                Break;
          default:
                default Statement;
                break;
    }
    next statement;
```

(*i*) Switch, case, default, are the keywords

(*ii*) Expression is any valid expression

(*iii*) Default part is optional

The following flow chart explains the working of the switch statement:

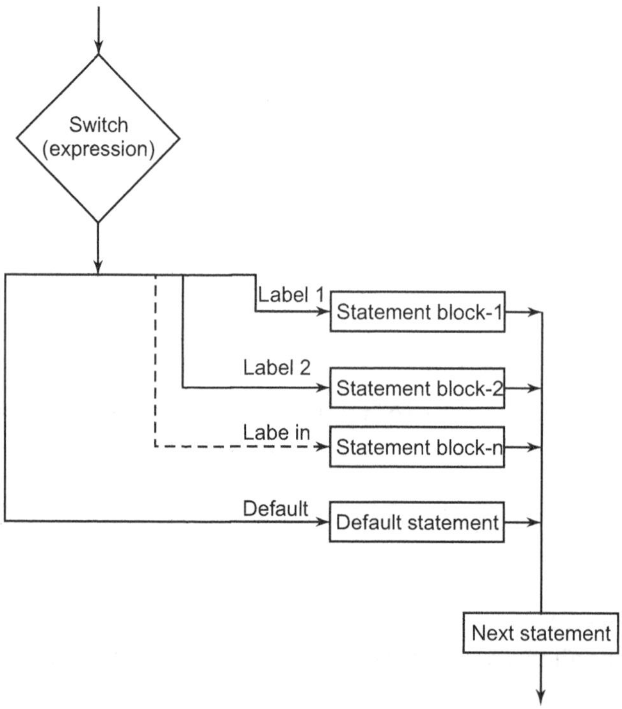

FIGURE 2.5

The switch statement works as follows:

1. Integer control expression is evaluated.
2. A match is looked for between this expression value and the case constants. If a match is found, execute the statements for that case. If a match is not found, execute the default statement.
3. Terminate switch when a break statement is encountered or by "falling out the end".

Example

```
#include<stdio.h>
main()
{

   int color;
   printf("enter the color number");
   scanf("%d", &color);
   switch(color)
     {
      case 1:
         printf("RED");
         break;
     case 2:
           printf("BLUE";);
           break;
     case 3:
           printf("GREEN");
                   break;
     default:
           printf("Invalid number");
           break;
            }
        }
     }
```

Compile and execute the above program
The output of the above program is shown here:
Enter color code[1.RED, 2.BLUE, 3.GREEN];
2
BLUE
Enter color code [1.RED, 2.BLUE, 3. GREEN];
5
Invalid Number

2.5.2. Looping Statement

Looping statement is used to execute a set of statements repeatedly until some condition is satisfied.

There are 3 types of looping statement. They are:

1. While loop statement
2. Do-while loop statement
3. For loop statement

2.5.2.1 While loop statement (Entry control statement)

The general format is

```
        while(test condition)
    {
         //body of the loop
    }
    next statement;
```

1. The computer first evaluates the loop condition.
2. If the value is true, then the body of the loop is executed repeatedly until the loop condition becomes false.
3. If the value is false, then control is transferred to the next statement.

The following flow chart explains the working of the while statement:

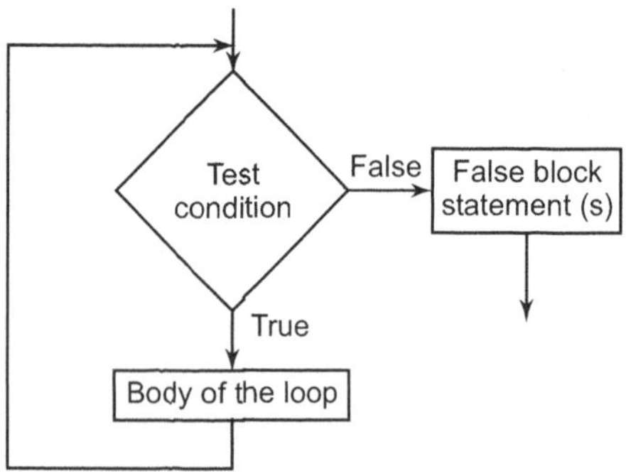

FIGURE 2.6

Example1

Write a C program to implement while loop

```
#include<stdio.h>
main()
{
    int i,n;
    printf("Enter the Number:");
    scanf("%d",&n);
    while(i<=n)
    {
```

```
   Printf"number=%d", i);
   i++;
  }
}
```

The output of the above program is shown here:

Enter the Number: 5

number=1

number=2

number=3

number=4

number=5

Example 2

Write a C to find the reversal of a given number

```
#include <stdio.h>
#include <conio.h>
int main()
{
   int num,rev=0;
   printf("enter the number to be reversed");
   scanf("%d", &num);
   while(num>0) //till the number is positive, perform the process
   {
   rev=rev*10 +(num%10);
   num=num/10;
}
printf("The reversal is %d ",rev);
 getch();
 return 0;
}
```

2.5.2.2 Do-while (Exit control statement)

The general format is

```
   do
   {
         //body of the loop;
   }
   while(test condition);
   next statement;
```

(*i*) Check the test condition

(*ii*) If it is true, execute the body of the loop.

(*iii*) If it is false, execute the next statement.

The following flow chart explains the working of the do-while statement

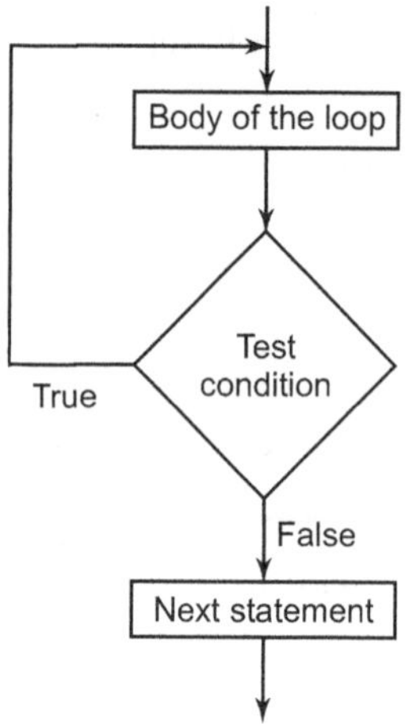

FIGURE 2.7

Example

Write a C Program to implement do-while loop.

```
#include<stdio.h>
main() {
    int i,n;
    printf("Enter the Number:");
    scanf("%d",&n);
    do    {
          printf"number=%d", i);
          i++;
        } while(i<=n);
}
```

The output of the above program is shown here:

Enter the Number: 5

number=1

number=2

number=3

number=4

number=5

Difference between while and do-while loop

Do-while	While
Condition is checked at the end of the loop	Condition is checked in the beginning of the loop.
Set of statements within the loop will be executed at least once.	If the condition fails the statements will not be executed even once.

2.5.2.3 for loop

For statement is used to execute a statement or a group of statements repeatedly for a number of times. The general form is:

```
for(initialization;testcondition;incredecrement)
{
   // body of the loop
}
next statement;
```

(*i*) Give the initial value to the control variable.

(*ii*) Check the test condition, If the test condition is true, execute the body of the loop.

(*iii*) If the test condition is false, execute the next statement.

The following flow chart explains the working of the for statement

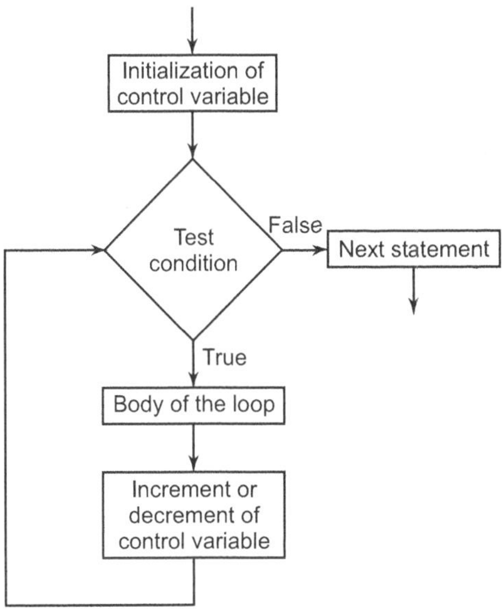

FIGURE 2.8

- The operation for the loop is as follows:
  1. The initialization expression is evaluated.
  2. The test expression is evaluated. If it is TRUE, body of the loop is executed. If it is FALSE, exit the for loop.

3. Assume test expression is TRUE. Execute the program statements making up the body of the loop.
4. Evaluate the increment expression and return to step 2.
5. When test expression is FALSE, exit loop and move on to next line of code.

Example

Write a C program to implement for loop

```
#include<stdio.h>
main()
{
 int i,n;
 printf("Enter the number");
 scanf("%d", &n);
 for(i=1;i<=10;i++)
  {
     printf("number=%d",i);
  }
 }
}
```

Compile and execute the above program

The output of the above program is shown here:

Enter the number

5

number = 1

number = 2

number = 3

number = 4

number = 5

2.5.3 Jump Statement

1. Break statement
2. Continue statement.

2.5.3.1 Break statement

Break statement is used to terminate from a loop while the test condition is true. This statement can be used with in a while do while, for and switch statement. The general format is:

```
break;
```

Example

```
for(i=0;i<20;i++)
{
        if(i==10)
        {
                break;
        }
}
```

2.5.3.2 Continue Statement

The continue statement is used to skip the remaining statement in the loop. It only works within loops where its effect is to force an immediate jump to the loop control statement.

- In a while loop, jump to the test statement.
- In a do while loop, jump to the test statement.
- In a for loop, jump to the test, and perform the iteration.

The general format is:

```
continue;
```

Example

```
int i;
for(i=0;i<10;i++)
{

if (i==5)
continue;
printf("%d",i);
if (i==8)
break;
}
```

This code will print 1 to 8 except 5.

Continue means, whatever code that follows the continue statement WITHIN the loop code block will not be executed and the program will go to the next iteration, in this case, when the program reaches i=5 it checks the condition in the if statement and executes 'continue', everything after continue, which are the printf statement, the next if statement, will not be executed.

Break statement will just stop execution of the look and go to the next statement after the loop if any. In this case when i=8 the program will jump out of the loop. Meaning, it won't continue till i=9, 10.

2.6 COMMA OPERATOR

A set of expressions separated by commas is a valid construct in the c language. For example, x and y are declared by the statement int x,y;

Consider the following statement that makes use of comma operator.

int a,b,c;

2.7 SAMPLE C PROGRAMS

Write a C program to check whether a number is Armstrong Number

The armstrong number is of the form 153= 13 + 53 + 33

The input is: 153 or any other number

Output: The number is armstrong or not.

Processing: take 153 as an example, remove 3, 5 and 1 in the reverse order (using % operator) and take the power of 3 and add to the sum variable.

If the total sum and the original number, both are same, then that is the armstrong number. If else, the number is not an armstrong number.

```
#include <stdio.h>
#include <conio.h>
int main()
{
    int original_num, check, temp, sum=0;
    printf("Enter the number to check for armstrong number");
    scanf("%d", &original_num);
    temp=original_num;
    while(original_num>0)
    {
          check=original_num%10; sum=sum+check*check*check; original_
          num=original_num/10;
    }
     if(sum==temp)
          printf("This is an armstrong number\n");
    else
          printf("This is not an armstrong number");
    getch();
    return 0;
}
```

Write a C program to check whether a given number is prime or not

A prime number can be divided by 1 and itself, there are no other divisors,

Examples are : 2 3, 5, 7, 11, ...

To find out whether a given number is prime or not, here is the logic

1. Get the number
2. Divide the given number from 2 to n-1 (Example if 6 is the number divided by 2,3,4,5 will get the remainder respectively 0,0,2,3)
3. Increment a counter to 1 if the remainder is 0
4. If there counter variable is 0, then the given number is prime (because we didn't get any remainder) else non prime

```
#include <stdio.h>
#include <conio.h>
int main()
{
        int a,i,count=0;
        printf("enter a"); //Let the given number is a
        scanf("%d",&a); //get the number
        for(i=2;i<a;i++)
        {
                if(a%i==0) count++;
        }
        if(count !=0)
        printf("a is not a prime number");
        else
        printf("a is a prime number");
        getch();
        return 0;
}
```

Write a C program to sort a Given set of numbers in ascending order (Bubble Sort)

/* Program to sort the given set of numbers in ascending order, this sorting is called as bubble sort algorithm */

```
#include <stdio.h>
#include <conio.h>
int main()
{
   int a[10],i,j,temp=0;
```

```
    printf("Enter all the 10 numbers");
    for(i=0;i<10;i++)
    scanf("%d",&a[i]);
    for(i=0;i<10;i++)
    {
            for(j=0;j<9;j++)
            {
            if(a[j]>a[j+1])
            {
                    temp=a[j];
                    a[j]=a[j+1];
                    a[j+1]=temp;
            }
    }
}
printf("The ordered array is");
for(j=0;j<10;j++) //Finally print the ordered array
printf("%d \t",a[j]);
getch();
return 0;
}
```

Write a C program to sort a set of numbers in the ascending order.

```
#include<stdio.h>
main()
{
    int i,j,k,n,l=1,arr[50],tmp;
    clrscr();
    printf("\t ASCENDING OF ORDERS\n");
    printf("\t~~~~~~~~~~~~~~~~~~~~~~");
    printf("\n Enter the number of elements to be
                                             sorted..");
    scanf("%d",&n);
    printf("\n Enter the elements to be sorted..");
    for(i=0;i<n;i++)
          scanf("%d",&arr[i]);
    for(i=0;i<n-1;i++)
    {
    for(j=i+1;j<n;j++)
```

```
    {
            if(arr[i]>arr[j])
            {
                    tmp=arr[i];
                    arr[i]=arr[j];
                    arr[j]=tmp;
            }
    }
    printf("\n Pass %d\n",l++);
    for(k=0;k<n;k++)
            printf("%d\t",arr[k]);
    }
    printf("\n\t Elements sorted in ascending
                                                order\n");
    for(i=0;i<n;i++)
    printf("\t %d\n",arr[i]);
    getch();
}
```

Write a C program for quadratic equation using pointers

```
#include<stdio.h>
#include<conio.h>
#include<math.h>
main()
{
    int a,b,c,*x,*y,*z;
    float temp,root1,root2;
    /*x=&a;
    y=&b;
    z=&c;*/
    clrscr();
    printf("\t QUADRATIC EQUATION (USING POINTERS)\n");
    printf("\t~~~~~~~~~~~~~~~~~~~~~~~~~~~~~~~~~~~~~~~\n");
    printf("Enter thecoefficients....:");
    scanf("%d%d%d",&a,&b,&c);
    if(a==0)
    {
            printf("Singleroot - Linear equation");
            root1=(float)-c/b;
            printf("\n The root of the equation is %5.2f",root1);
    }
    else
    temp=b*b-4*a*c;
    if(temp<0)
            {
            printf("\n Imaginary roots");
            temp=-temp;
            temp=(float)(sqrt(temp));
            root1=(float)-b/(2*a);
```

```
        printf("\n The real part is % 5.2f",root1);
        printf("\n The imaginary part is (%5.2f)i/%d",temp,2*a);
        }
  else
        if(temp>0)
  {
  printf("\n Real roots");
  root1=(float)(-b+sqrt(b*b-4*a*c))/(2*a);
  root2=(float)(-b-sqrt(b*b-4*a*c))/(2*a);
  printf("\n The roots of the equation are %5.2f and
  %5.2f",root1,root2);
        }
  else
        {
        printf("\n Single real root\n");
        root1=-b/(2*a);
        printf("\n the roots of the equation is %5.2f",root1);
        }
  getch();
  }
```

Write a C program for print customer name and type of product and discount, bill amount.

```
#include<stdio.h>
#include<conio.h>
#define FIVE 0.0F
#define SEVEN 0.075
#define TEN 0.1
#define FTEEN 0.15
main()
{
   float amt,disc,total;
   int type,ch=0;
   char name[20];
   float mill(float);
   float handloom(float);
   clrscr();
   do
   {
   printf("Enter the customer's name; ");
   gets(name);
   printf("\n Enter the amount purchased by the
                                customer..Rs.");
   scanf("%f",&amt);
   printf("\n Enter the type purchased (0-mill&1-handloom:");
   scanf("%d",&type);
   switch(type) {
   case 0:
```

```
          disc=mill(amt);
          break;
    case 1:
          disc=handloom(amt);
          break;
    }
    total=amt-disc;
    clrscr();
    printf("\t\t CASH BILL\n");
    printf("\t\t ~~~~~~~~~~\n");
    printf("\n\t customer's Name  :%s",name);
    if(type==0)
    printf("\n\t The cloth type is Mill\n\n");
    else
    printf("\n\t The cloth type is Handloom\n\n");

    printf("\n\t The amount purchased is
                                Rs.%6.2f",amt);
    printf("\n\t The amount of discount is
                               Rs.%6.2f",disc);
    printf("\n\t The amount to be paid is
                           Rs.%6.2f\n\n",total);
    printf("\n\t~~~~~~~~~~~~~~~~~~~~~~~~~~~~~~\n\n");
    printf("\n\n continue ? (0--> yes, 1-->no):");
    scanf("%d",&ch);
    clrscr();
    }while(ch!=1);
}
float mill(float sum){
float d;
    if(sum<=100)
          d=0.0;
    else if(sum<=200)
          d=FIVE*sum;
    else if(sum<=300)
          d=SEVEN*sum;
    else
          d=TEN*sum;
    return(d); }
    float handloom(float sum){
    float d;
    if(sum<=100)
          d=FIVE*sum;
    else if(sum<=200)
          d=SEVEN*sum;
    else if(sum<=300)
          d=TEN*sum;
    else
          d=FTEEN*sum;
return(d);
}
```

Write a C program to Count the number of vowels, consonants, words, white spaces in a line of text and array of lines.

```
#include<stdio.h>
#include<conio.h>
main()
{
   char s[50];
   int i,c=0,w=1,v=0,len;
   clrscr();
   printf("\nEnter the text: ");
   gets(s);
   len=strlen(s);
   for(i=0;i<len;i++)
   {
    switch(toupper(s[i]))
    {
      case 'A':
      case 'E':
      case 'I':
      case 'O':
      case 'U': v++; break;
      case ' ': w++; break;
      default : c++; break;
    }
   }
      printf("\nThe given text: %s",s);
      printf("\nThe no. of vowels: %d",v);
      printf("\nThe no. of consonant: %d",c);
      printf("\nThe no. of words: %d",w);
      printf("\nThe no. of spaces: %d",w-1);
      getch();
   }
```

Write a C program to reverse a given string and check whether the given string is palindrome or not.

```
#include<stdio.h>
#include<string.h>
main()
{
   char str[80],rev[80];
   int i,j,len;
   clrscr();
   printf("\n\t\t\t\PALINDROME CHECKING");
   printf("\n\t\t\t\t------------------");
   printf("\n\nEnter the string\n\n");
   gets(str);
   len=strlen(str);
```

```
    for(i=len-1,j=0;i>=0;i--,j++)
    rev[j]=str[i];
    rev[j]='\0';
    printf("\nThe original string:%s",str);
    printf("\nThe reversed string:%s\n\n\n\n",rev);
    if(strcmp(str,rev)==0)
       printf("%s is a palindrome",str);
    else
      printf("%s is not a palindrome",str);
    getch();
}
```

Write a C program to implement linear search

```
#include<stdio.h>
   #include<conio.h>
   main()
   {
        int a[]={12,27,5,83,94,36,72,11,54,43};
        int i=0,n=10,x,found=0;
        clrscr();
        printf("\n Enter a Number to search : ");
        scanf("%d",&x);
        while(i<n&&!found)
        if(a[i++]==x)
        found=1;
        found?
        printf("\t%d : is found",x):printf("\t%d: not
                                               found",x);
        getch();
   }
```

LET US SUMMARISE

- The getchar() function reads a single character from the keyboard.
- The putchar() function displays a single character on the screen.
- The printf ( ) function is used to display values or results at the terminal.
- The gets ( ) function is used to read a string form the keyboard until a carriage return key is pressed.
- The puts( ) function outputs the string of characters stored in variable on the screen.
- Control statements are used to transfer control from one statement to any other statement in a program.

REVIEW QUESTIONS

1. Define Control Statements.
2. What is Loop?
3. Define Break and Continue Statement.

4. Write the syntax of switch statement.
5. Write the syntax of if-else statement.
6. What is the purpose of comma operator?

EXERCISES

1. Write a C Program to check whether the given number is even or odd.
2. Write a C Program to check whether the given number is multiple of 7 or not.
3. Write a C Program to manipulate student result. i.e. either pass or fail. Accept three subject marks from user.
4. Write a C Program to display 1 to 'n' numbers using while loop.
5. Write a C Program to find reverse of a given number.
6. Write a C Program to display first 'n' numbers using do-while loop.
7. Write a C Program to find sum of first 'n' numbers.
8. Write a C Program to check whether the given number is prime or not.

CHAPTER 3

FUNCTIONS AND STORAGE CLASSES

3.1 FUNCTIONS

Functions are the building blocks of the C programming language. The most important of the c functions is the main () function. A function can be invoked from different parts of the main program.

In C language, there are two different types of functions. They are:

1. Library functions
2. User defined functions

1. Library Functions

Library Functions are functions not to be written by the programmer. But these are available in separate files called header files. The commonly used predefined functions are as follows:

(*i*) String function(string.h) or string handling functions.

(*ii*) Math function(math.h)

2. User defined functions

A user defined function has to be written by the programmer to carry out some specific well defined task.

A function in C is a small "sub-program" that performs a particular task, and supports the concept of modular programming design techniques. In modular programming the various tasks that your overall program must accomplish are assigned to individual functions and the main program basically calls these functions in a certain order.

3.1.1 Need for User Defined Functions

- Length of source program can be reduced by using user defined functions.
- Faulty functions can be easily located.
- User defined functions can be used in any "C" program.

A Function should be defined before it is used. A function has two parts. Namely,

1. Function header
2. Statement body

Declaration of function

The general format is

```
Function header ——→ return type function_name(list of arguments
                                  argument declaration)

                        {     Local declaration;
                              Executable statement;
                              ----------------------
Statement body
                              ---------------------
                        }     Executable statement;
                              return(expression);
```

Where,

Function type	- data type of the value returned by the function.
Function name	- name of the function
List of argument	- parameters
Argument declaration	- declaration of formal argument
Return	- return the value of the function to other function.

Rules

- Function header should not terminate with semicolon.
- List of argument and declaration and return is optional.

3.2 RETURN STATEMENT

A function returns a value to the calling program with the use of the keyword return, followed by a data variable or constant value. The return statement can even contain an expression. The general format is

```
return or return(expression);
```

For Example

```
return 3;
return n;
return (a*b);
```

- When a return is encountered the following events occur:
    1. Execution of the function is terminated and control is passed back to the calling program.
    2. The function call evaluates to the value of the *return expression*.
- If there is no return statement control is passed back when the closing brace of the function is encountered.

3.3 FUNCTION PROTOTYPE

Function prototype means, declaring the defined function in the main program. The general format is

```
datatype function_name( );
```

where,

datatype – valid c data type.

Function_name - name of the function

3.4 CALLING A FUNCTION

A defined function can be called from other functions by specifying its name followed by a list of arguments enclosed within parentheses. The general form is

```
Function_name(list of arguments);
```

Rules

- Function_name should be the name used in the function definition.
- list of argument is optional.

Example 1

```
#include<stdio.h>
main()
{
        int a,b;
        int abc();◄──────── function prototype
        scanf("%d%d", &a,&b);
        printf("%d", abc(a,b));
                      ▲
}                     └──────── function calling
int abc(I,j)
int I,j;
{
        int k;
        k=i+j;
        retrun(k);
}
```

Example 2

```
#include<stdio.h>
main()
{
        int mul(int a,int b);
        {
                Int c;
                C=a*b;
                Return(c)
        }
```

```
main()
{
        int x,y,z;
        x=5;
        y=10;
        c=mul(x,y);
        printf("the value of c is %d", c);
}
```

3.5 FORMAL AND ACTUAL ARGUMENTS

3.5.1 Formal Arguments

The arguments present in the function definition are called formal arguments. These are also called as dummy arguments.

Example

```
int abc(I,j)
int I,j;
{
        int k;
        k=i+j;
        retrun(k);
}
```

In this function I and j are called formal or dummy arguments because the values for the arguments I and j are not available.

3.5.2 Passing Arguments

The arguments present in the function calling are called passing arguments or actual arguments.

Example

```
main()
{
        int x,y,z;
        x=5;
        y=10;
        c=mul(x,y);
        printf("the value of c is %d", c);
}
```

In the above example, x and y are called actual or passing arguments, because only through this the called function mul receives the values of the formal arguments I and j as 5 and 10.

3.6 CATEGORY OF FUNCTIONS/TYPES OF FUNCTION

There are four types of functions. They are:

1. Function with no arguments and no return value.

2. Function with arguments and no return value.
3. Function with no arguments and return value.
4. Function with arguments and return value.

3.6.1 Function with no Arguments and no Return Value

This is the simplest function. This does not receive any arguments from the calling function and does not return any value to the calling function.

3.6.2 Function with Arguments and no Return Value

This function receives arguments from the calling function and does not return any value to the calling function.

3.6.3 Function with no Arguments and Return Value

This function does not receive arguments from the calling function and return the computed value back to the calling function.

3.6.4 Function with Arguments and Return Value

This function receives arguments from the calling program and return the computed value back to the calling function.

3.7 RECURSION

A recursive function is one that calls itself again and again. Recursive functions are useful in evaluating certain types of mathematical function. You may also encounter certain dynamic data structures such as linked lists or binary trees. Recursion is a very useful way of creating and accessing these structures.

Example

Write a program to find the factorial of a given number.

```
#include<stdio.h>
main()
{
        Int fact(int n);
        Int I,a;
        Scanf("%d", &i);
        A=fact(i);
        Printf("%d", a);
}
int fact(int n)
{
        Int f;
        If(n==0)
        return 1;
        else
        f=n*fact(n-1);
        return(f);
}
```

Explanation

Let us assume n=4, since the value of n is not equal to 0 the statement,

Fact = n*fact(n-1)

```
Call – 1
                    Fact=4*fact(3)
Call – 2
                    Fact=4*3*fact(3)
Call – 3
                    Fact=4*3*2*fact(3)
Call – 4
                    Fact=4*3*2*1*fact(3)
Call – 5
                    Fact=4*3*2*1
Factorial 4 = 24
```

3.8 STORAGE CLASSES

A storage class defined both scope and life time of identifiers. The default storage class is auto, which declares the scope of the variable as local.

Types of storage classes

The various types of storage classes are as follows:

1. Automatic
2. External
3. Register
4. Static

1. **Automatic:** This is the default storage class for the local variables. The variable which are declared inside a function are called automatic variable. The general format is

```
auto datatype variabel, variabe2,...... variable n;
```

Example

```
auto int a,b;
```

2. **External:** The variable which are declared outside the functions are called external variable, Since these variables are not declared within a specific function, these are common to all the functions in the program. The general format is

```
extern datatype variable1, variable2,...... variable n;
```

Example

```
extern int a;
```

3. **Register:** The variable which are stored in the registered are called register variable. The general format is

```
register datatype variable1, variable2,...... variable n;
```

Example

```
register in b;
```

4. **Static:** Static variables are variables which retain the values till the end of the program. The general format is

```
static datatype variable1, variable2,...... variable n;
```

Example

```
static in a,b;
```

LET US SUMMARISE

- Functions are the building blocks of the C programming language.
- Library Functions are functions not to be written by the programmer.
- A user defined function has to be written by the programmer to carry out some specific well defined task.
- A function send value to the calling using return statement.
- Function prototype means, declaring the defined function in the main program.
- A defined function can be called from other functions by specifying its name followed by a list of arguments enclosed within parentheses.
- The arguments present in the function definition are called formal arguments. These are also called as dummy arguments.
- The arguments present in the function calling are called passing arguments or actual arguments.

REVIEW QUESTIONS

1. What is Function?
2. List out the part of functions?
3. Define storage class.
4. Define Recursion.
5. What is function prototype?

EXERCISES

1. Write a C program to define user-defined functions. Call them at different places.
2. Write a C program to use return statement in different ways.
3. Write a C program to send value to user defined function and display results.

CHAPTER 4

ARRAYS AND STRUCTURES AND UNION

4.1 ARRAYS

Arrays are widely used data type in 'C' language Array is a group of related data items, that share a common name with same data type. An individual variable in the array is called an array element.

We can define an arrayname,rollno to represent a set of rollno of a group of students. A particular value is indicated by a number called index number. An index number is present in brackets after the arrayname.

- One Dimensional Array
- Two Dimensional Array
- Multidimensional Array

4.1.1 One Dimensional Array

A list of items group in a single variable name with only one index is called 1- D array.

Declaration and initialization of arrays

(*i*) **Declaration of One Array:** We can declare an array in C using subscript operator. The general form is

```
datatype var_name[size];
```

Here, datatype is valid c datatype and var_name is the name of the array.

Example

i) `int mark[50];`

This declares an integer type array names as mark having 50 memory locations to store 100 integer data.

ii) `float salary[30];`

This declares a floating point type array named as salary having 30 memory locations to store 30 floating point data.

```
iii) char name[20];
```

This declares a character type array named as name having 20 memory locations to store 20 characters.

(*ii*) **Initialization of 1-D Arrays:** We can store values at the time of declaration. The compiler allocates the required space depending upon the list of values. The general form is :

```
datatype array_name[size] = { list of values};
```

Example 1

```
i) int mark[4]={45,58,90,76};
```

This declare mark as an integer array having four locations and assign initial values as given below.

mark[0]	mark[1]	mark[2]	mark[3]
45	58	90	76

```
ii) int mark[6];
```

If the size of the array is greater than the number of values in the list, then the unused locations are filled with zeros as given below

mark[0]	mark[1]	mark[2]	mark[3]	mark[4]	mark[5]
45	58	90	76	0	0

```
iii) char dept[10];
```

This declares name as a character array having 10 characters and assign initial values as

dept[0]	dept[1]	dept[2]	dept[3]	dept[4]	dept[5]	dept[6]	dept[7]
C	O	P	U	T	E	R	\0

4.1.2 Two Dimensional Arrays

A list of items group in a single variable name with two indexes (row and column size) is called 2-D array.

(*i*) **Creation of 2-D Arrays:** We can create two dimensional array as follows:

```
datatype arrayname[size1][size2];
```

Here,

`size1` – number of rows

`size2` – number of columns

Example

```
i) int   arr[2 ] [ 3];
```

This represents a two dimensional array named arr.

Structure of two-dimensional arrays as shown here:

arr[0][0]	arr[0][1]	arr[0][2]
arr[1][0]	arr[1][1]	arr[1][2]

```
ii) int mark[5][2];
```

This declares mark as a two dimensional integer array having 5 rows and 2 columns. The total number of locations is 5x2 = 10.

	columns	**column1**
row0	mark[0][0]	mark[0][1]
row1	mark[1][0]	mark[1][1]
row2	mark[2][0]	mark[2][1]
row3	mark[3][0]	mark[3][1]
row4	mark[4][0]	mark[4][1]

(*ii*) **Initialization of 2-D Arrays:** Two dimensional array can be initialized similar to one dimensional array as below.

```
datatype arrayname[size1][size2]={list of values};
```

Example

(*i*) int mark[3][2]={45,65,89,78,99,66};

mark[0][0]	mark[0][1]
45	65
mark[1][0]	mark[1][1]
89	78
mark[2][0]	mark[2][1]
99	66

4.1.3 Multidimensional Arrays

Three or more dimensional arrays can also be used in C. The general form is

```
dataype  arrayname[size1][size2],[size3]........[size n];
```

Example

```
int  mark[5][4][3][2];
```

In the above example mark is a four dimensional array to store 120 integer type of data.

4.1.4 Sample C Programs

Write a C program to search a number in a given array

```
//This program is to search a given number in an array
#include <stdio.h>
#include <conio.h>
int main()
{
   int a[10],i,num;
```

```
   printf("enter the array elements");
   for(i=0;i<10;i++) //get all the numbers
   scanf("%d",&a[i]);
   printf("Enter the number to search");
    scanf("%d",&num);
 for(i=0;i<10;i++)
 {
   if(a[i]==num) //given num is matched in the array
 {
 printf("The number is found in the %d position",i+1);
 getch();
 exit(0); //to go the end of the program
 }
}
 printf("The number is not found");
 getch();
return 0;
}
```

Write a C program to add two matrices

```
/* Program to add two matrices */
#include <stdio.h>
#include <conio.h>
int main()
{
   int a[10][10], b[10][10],c[10][10],i,j;
   printf("Enter a");
   for(i=0;i<2;i++) //get the matrix A
   for(j=0;j<2;j++)
   scanf("%d",&a[i][j]);
   printf("Enter b");
   for(i=0;i<2;i++) //get the matrix B
   for(j=0;j<2;j++)
   scanf("%d",&b[i][j]);
   for(i=0;i<2;i++)
   {
   for(j=0;j<2;j++)
   {
   c[i][j] = a[i][j] +b[i][j]; //adding two matrices
   }
}
printf("Added Matrix is \n");
for(i=0;i<2;i++)
for(j=0;j<2;j++)
printf("%d ",c[i][j]);
getch();
return 0;
}
```

Write a C program to multiply two matrices

```
/* Program to multiply two matrices */
#include <stdio.h>
#include <conio.h>
int main()
{
   int a[2][3],b[3][2],c[2][2],k,j,i;
   printf("enter a");
   for(i=0;i<2;i++) //Get array A
   {
   for(j=0;j<3;j++)
   {
   scanf("%d",&a[i][j]);
}
}
printf("enter b");
for(i=0;i<3;i++) //Get array B
{
   for(j=0;j<2;j++)
   {
         scanf("%d",&b[i][j]);
   }
}
   for(i=0;i<2;i++)
    {
         for(j=0;j<2;j++)
         {
         c[i][j]=0;
         for(k=0;k<3;k++)
         {
           c[i][j]=c[i][j]+a[i][k]*b[k][j];
         }
   }
}
printf("C is ");
for(i=0;i<2;i++)
for(j=0;j<2;j++)
printf(" c[%d][%d] – %d \n",i,j,c[i][j]);
getch();
return 0;
}
```

Write a C program to create a 3*3*3 matrix and find the sum of matrix.

```
#include<stdio.h>
main()
{
      static int num[3][3][3],i,j,k,sum=0,l=1;
     clrscr();
     for(i=0;i<3;i++)
```

```
    for(j=0;j<3;j++)
    for(k=0;k<3;k++)
    {
      num[i][j][k]=l;
      l++;
      sum+=num[i][j][k];
      }
      printf("\n\t\tTHREE DIMENSIONAL ARRAY");
      printf("\n\t\t*************************\n\n");
      for(i=0;i<3;i++)
      {
        for(j=0;j<3;j++)
        {
          for(k=0;k<3;k++)
          {
          printf("\t\t%d",num[i][j][k]);
          }
          printf("\n");
          }
          printf("\n");
        }
      printf("\n\tThe sum of the elements of the array is
                                           :%d\n",sum);
      getch();
}
```

4.2 STRUCTURE

A structure is a collection of variables under a single name. These variables can be of different types, and each has a name which is used to select it from the structure. A structure is a convenient way of grouping several pieces of related information together.

4.2.1 Defining Structure

A structure definition contains a keyword struct and a user defined tag-field. The general format is,

```
struct tag-field
{
      datatype member1;
      datatype member2;
      ---------------------
      ---------------------
      datatype member1;
};
```

Where,

`Struct`	- keyword to define structure
`Tag-field`	- name of the structure
`Datatype`	- valid c datatype

Example

Below structure can be defined for storing book details of a book store.

```
struct book_store
{
        char title[15];
        char author[15];
        int pages;
        float price;
}
```

This defines a structure with four members namely, title, author, pages and price of different data types. The name of the structure is book_store.

4.2.2 Structure Declaration

Structure declaration means combining template declarations and variable declarations. The general format is

struct tag-filed variable1, variable2,......... variablen;

Example

```
struct book_store
{
        char title[15];
        char author[15];
        int pages;
        float price;
        struct book_store book1,book2,book3;
}
```

4.2.3 Giving Values to Structure Members

Member operator or dot operator is used to establish a link between member in a structure an structure variable.(' . '). The general format is

```
structure variable . membername;
```

Example

```
#include<stdio.h>
struct book_store
{
        Char title[15];
        Char author[15];
        Int pages;
        Float price;
};
main()
{
        struct book_store book1;
        printf("input values");
scanf("%c%c%d%f",&book1.title,&book1.author,&book1.pages,
                                                    &book1.price);
```

```
        Printf("%c%c%d%f",book1.title,book1.author,book1.pages,
        book1.price);
}
```

4.2.4 Structure Initialization

Structure variable can be initialized similar to other data types in C. The general format is

static struct tag-filed structure variable={ list of values};

Example

```
struct book_store
{
        Char title[15];
        Char author[15];
        Int pages;
        Float price;
}static book1={ " Programming in C", " Rizwan",230,85};
```

4.2.5 Difference Between Arrays and Structure

Arrays	Structure
All data in an array should be of same data type.	Structures data can be of different data type.
Individual entries in an array are called elements.	Structure individual entries are called members.

4.3 STRUCTURES WITHIN STRUCTURES

Structures can have as members other structures. A structure that contained both date and time information. One way to accomplish this would be to combine two separate structures; one for the date and one for the time.

For Example

```
struct date
{
        int month;
        int day;
        int year;
};
struct time
{
int hour;
        int min;
        int sec;
};
struct date_time
{
```

```
        struct date today;
        struct time now;
    };
```

This declares a structure whose elements consist of two other previously declared structures. Initialization could be done as follows:

```
static struct date_time veteran =
            {11,11,2011},{11,11,11}};
```

which sets the **today** element of the structure **veteran** to the eleventh of November, 2011. The **now** element of the structure is initialized to eleven hours, eleven minutes, eleven seconds. Each item within the structure can be referenced if desired.

4.4 POINTERS TO STRUCTURES

One can have pointer variable that contain the address of complete structures, just like with the basic data types. Structure pointers are declared and used in the same manner as "simple" pointers:

```
struct playing_card *card_pointer,down_card;
card_pointer=&down_card;
(*card_pointer).pips=8;
```

The above code has **indirectly initialized** the structure **down_card** to the Eight of Clubs through the use of the pointer **card_pointer**. (*card_pointer).suit="Clubs";

The type of the variable card_pointer is "pointer to a playing_card structure".

In C, there is a special symbol **->** which is used as a shorthand when working with pointers to structures. It is officially called the **structure pointer operator**. Its syntax is as follows:

(struct_ptr).member is the same as ***struct_ptr->member***

Thus, the last two lines of the previous example could also have been written as: .

```
card_pointer->pips=8;
card_pointer->suit="Clubs";
```

4.5 SELF-REFERENTIAL STRUCTURE

A self referential structure is used to create data structures like linked lists, stacks, etc. Following is an example of this kind of structure:

```
struct struct_name
{
        datatype datatypename;
        struct_name * pointer_name;
};
```

A self-referential structure is one of the data structures which refer to the pointer to (points) to another structure of the same type. For example, a linked list is supposed to be a self-referential data structure. The next node of a node is being pointed, which is of the same struct type. For example,

```
typedef struct listnode {
void *data;
struct listnode *next;
} linked_list;
```

Sample C Program

/*program for student mark statement */

```
#include<stdio.h>
#include<conio.h>
#include<string.h>
struct stud
   {
   char name[20];
   int score[10];
   int high;
   int low;
   float aveg;
   char grade;
 }cand;
main()
{
input();
output();
}
input()
{
int j,sum,mk;
float avgmk;
clrscr();
printf("\n\t\t ABC SCHOOL OF STUDIES::CHENNAI\n\n");
printf("\n Enter the name..");
scanf("%s",&cand.name);
printf("\nEnter the 10 test marks..\n");
cand.low=100;
cand.high=0;
sum=0;
for(j=0;j<5;j++)
   {
   printf("test %d:",j+1);
   scanf("%d",&mk);
   cand.score[j]=mk;
   sum+=mk;
   if(cand.high<mk)
         cand.high=mk;
   if(cand.low>mk)
         cand.low=mk;
   }
   avgmk=sum/5.0;
   cand.aveg=avgmk;
   if(avgmk<40)
         cand.grade='F';
   else
         if(avgmk<50)
               cand.grade='D';
         else
```

```
                if(avgmk<60)
                        cand.grade='C';
                else
                        if(avgmk<75)
                                cand.grade='B';
                        else
                                cand.grade='A';
    }
    /* output printing */
    output()
    {
        int j;
        clrscr();
        printf("\n\t\t ABC SCHOOL OF STUDIES::CHENNI\n");
        printf("\t\t______________________________\n");
        printf("\n NAME :%s\n",cand.name);
        for(j=0;j<5;j++)
        printf("\n\t test %d     :%d",j+1,cand.score[j]);
        printf("\n\n\n\t\tHighest     :%d",cand.high);
        printf("\n\t\tLowest     :%d",cand.low);
        printf("\n\t\tAverage    :%5.2f",cand.aveg);
        printf("\n\t\tGrade      :%c\n",cand.grade);
        getch();
    }
```

4.6 UNION

Unions are derived data type. Union data type is similar to structure. The main advantage of union is they conserve memory. A union is a single piece of memory that is shared by two or more variables.

4.6.1 Declaration of Union

The union can be declared in the same way as the definition of structure. The general format is

```
union tag-filed
{
        Datatype member1;
        Datatype member2;
        ----------------------
        ----------------------
        Datatype membern;
}
```

Example

```
union student
{
        Int rollno;
        Char name[12];
}std;
```

Example

```
#include<stdio.h>
main()
{
        struct bio
        {
                char name[15];
                int rollno;
        }std;
        union bio_data
        {
                char name[15];
                int rollno;
        }bi;
        printf(" Enter the name and rollno");
        scanf("%c%d", &name,&rollno);
        printf("name=%d", std.name);
        printf("rollno=%d",std.rollno);
        printf("name=%d",bi.name);
        printf("rollno=%d",bi.rollno);
}
```

4.7 DIFFERENCE BETWEEN STRUCTURE AND UNION

Structure	Union
Structure: The size in bytes is the sum total of size of all the elements in the structure, plus padding bytes.	Size of in bytes of the union is size of the largest variable element in the union.

Size Allocated to a Structure:
For eg:
`struct example`
`{`
`int integer;`
`float floating_numbers;`
`}`
the size allocated here is eof(int)+sizeof(float);
where as in an union
	Size Allocated to a Union:
	For eg:
	`union example`
	`{`
	`int integer;`
	`float floating_numbers;`
	`}`
	size allocated is the size of the highest member.
	so size is=sizeof(float);

Advantage of union over structure

->Less RAM space is required thus fast execution of program.

Disadvantage of union over structure

->If we use 2 or more instance of single union the data will be lost after data for second instance is entered.

4.8 BITWISE OPERATIONS

C provides six operators for bit manipulation; these may only be applied to integral operands, that is, char , short , int , and long. The bitwise operators of C a summarized in the following table:

Table: Bitwise Operators

&	**Bitwise AND**
|	Bitwise Inclusive OR
^	Bitwise exclusive XOR
~	One's Compliment
<<	Left shift
>>	Right Shift

Do not confuse & with &&: & is bitwise AND, && logical AND. Similarly for | and ||.

~ is a unary operator -- it only operates on one argument to right of the operator.

The shift operators perform appropriate shift by operator on the right to the operator on the left. The right operator must be positive. The vacated bits are filled with zero (i.e. There is **NO** wrap around).

For example: *x* << 2 shifts the bits in *x* by 2 places to the left.

So:

if *x* = 00000010 (binary) or 2 (decimal)

then: x>>=2>➔x=00000000 or 0 (decimal)

Also: if *x* = 00000010 (binary) or 2 (decimal)

X<<=2➔00001000 or 8 (decimal)

Therefore a shift left is equivalent to a multiplication by 2.

Similarly a shift right is equal to division by 2.

To illustrate many points of bitwise operators let us write a function, Bit count, that counts bits set to 1 in an 8 bit number (unsigned char) passed as an argument to the function.

```
int bitcount(unsigned char x)
{
        int count;
        for (count=0; x != 0; x>>=1)
        if ( x & 01)
        count++;
        return count;
}
```

This function illustrates many C program points:

- For loop not used for simple counting operation
- x>>=1 ➔ x = x >> 1
- For loop will repeatedly shift right x until x becomes 0
- Use expression evaluation of x & 01 to control if
- x & 01 *masks* of 1st bit of x if this is 1 then count++

Bit Fields

Bit Fields allow the packing of data in a structure. This is especially useful when memory or data storage is at a premium. Typical examples:

- Packing several objects into a machine word. *e.g.* 1 bit flags can be compacted -- Symbol tables in compilers.
- Reading external file formats -- non-standard file formats could be read in. *e.g.* 9 bit integers.

C lets us do this in a structure definition by putting: bit *length* after the variable. *i.e.*

```
struct packed_struct
 {
    unsigned int f1:1;
    unsigned int f2:1;
    unsigned int f3:1;
    unsigned int f4:1;
    unsigned int type:4;
    unsigned int funny_int:9;
} pack;
```

Here the packed_struct contains 6 members: Four 1 bit *flags* f1..f3, a 4 bit type and a 9 bit funny_int.

4.9 USER DEFINED DATA TYPE

C Language supports a feature known as "type definition" that allows users to define an identifier that would represent an existing data type. The user defined data type identifier can later be used to declare variables. It takes the general form:

```
typedef type identifier;
```

Eg: typedef int units;

LET US SUMMARISE

- Array is a group of related data items, that share a common name with same data type.
- A list of items group in a single variable name with only one index is called 1- D array.
- A list of items group in a single variable name with two indexes (row and column size) is called 2-D array.
- A structure definition contains a keyword struct and a user defined tag-filed.
- Structure is a collection of various data types. Or it is defined as a data type to represent several different types of data with a single name.
- Structure declaration means combining template declarations and variable declarations.
- Member operator or dot operator is used to establish a link between member in a structure an structure variable.(' . ').
- A self referential structure is used to create data structures like linked lists, stacks, etc
- Unions are derived data type. Union data type is similar to structure. The main advantage of union is they conserve memory.

REVIEW QUESTIONS

1. What is arrays?
2. Define one dimensional arrays.
3. Define 2-D array.
4. How to initialize 1-D array?
5. Define Structure.
6. What is union?
7. Difference between Structure and Union.

EXERCISES

1. Write a C Program to display character array with their address.
2. Write a C Program to print string in the reverse order.
3. Write a C program to define a structure and initialize its number variables.

CHAPTER 5

POINTERS AND FILES

5.1 POINTERS

A pointer is a variable which contains the address in memory of another variable. Or A pointer is a data object that contains the address of another object.

Pointer declaration

A pointer is a variable that contains the memory location of another variable in which data is stored. Using pointer, you start by specifying the type of data stored in the location. The asterisk helps to tell the compiler that you are creating a pointer variable. Finally, you have to give the name of the variable. The address operator & is used to get the address of any data object and it is stored in pointer type data object.

5.1.1 Accessing the Address of the Variable

The address operator & is used to get the address of any data object and it is stored in pointer type data object.

```
P=& quantity
```

In this statement, the address of variable memory quantity (5000) is assigned to the pointer variable p.

Example

```
#include<stdio.h>
main()
{
    char a;
    Int s;
    float b;
    a='R';
    s=100;
    b=14.75;
    printf("%c is stored at address %u\n",a,&a);
    printf("%d is stored at address %u\n",a,&s);
    printf("%f is stored at address %u\n",a,&b);
}
```

The output of the above program is as follows:

R is stored at address 5083

100 is stored at address 5076

14.75 is stored at address 5041

5.1.2 Declaring and Initializing Pointers

The address of a variable can be stored in another variable called the pointer variable. Pointer variable can be declared as below:

```
Datatype * pointer variable name;
```

Example

```
Int *p;
```

In the above example, the declaration p is declared as pointer variable denoting integer data type. P can be made to point an integer variable using assignment statement.

P=&quantity;

In this example the address of variable quantity is assigned to p. This is called pointer initialization.

5.1.3 Accessing a Variable Through its Pointer

After assigning the address of a variable to a pointer variable that variable value can be accessed the pointer variable using the unary operator*(asterisk) as below:

```
Int quantity,*p,n;
Quantity=150;
P=&quantity;
N=*p;
```

In the above example, the two statements,

P=&quantity;

N=*p;

Are equivalent to n=*&quantity(or) n=quantity.

5.1.4 Pointer Operators

C provides two special pointer operators to manipulate the data items directly form the memory location.

- Address operator (&) –The address operator & gives the ``address of a variable".
- Indirection operator(*) - The indirection or dereference operator * gives the ``contents of an object pointed to by a pointer".

5.2 OPERATIONS ON POINTERS

Pointer Arithmetic and Pointer Expression

Pointer variables can be used in expression of C language similar to other variables. For example let us assume p1 and p2 are declared as pointer variable and are initialized.

```
Y=*p1 *p2→(*p1)(*p2)
```

In expressions, like other variables pointer variables can be used. For example if p1 and p2 are properly initialized and declared pointers, then the following statements are valid.

```
y=*p1**p2;
sum=sum+*p1;
z= 5* – *p2/p1;
*p2= *p2 + 10;
```

C allows us to subtract integers to or add integers from pointers as well as to subtract one pointer from the other. We can also use shorthand operators with pointers p1+=; sum+=*p2; etc., By using relational operators, we can also compare pointers like the expressions such as p1 >p2 , p1==p2 and p1!=p2 are allowed.

Example

/* a programs to display the memory address of a variable using pointer and to add with an integer quantity with pointer and to display the content of the pointer */

```
#include<stdio.h>
main()
{
    int x;
    int *ptr1,*ptr2;
    x=10;
    ptr1=&x;
    ptr2=ptr1+6;
    printf("value of x=%d\n",x);
    printf("content of ptr1=%d\n",*ptr1);
    printf("address of ptr1=%u\n",ptr1);
    printf("adress of ptr2=(ptr+6)=%u\n",ptr2);
    printf("contents of ptr2=%d\n",*ptr2);
}
```

/* end */value of x=10

content of ptr1=10

address of ptr1=65496

address of ptr2=(ptr+6)=65508

contents of ptr2=-24

5.3 ARRAYS OF POINTERS

The way there can be array of int's or an array of floats, similarly, there can be an arrays of pointers. Since a pointer variable always contains an address, an array of pointers would be nothing but a collection of addresses. The addresses present in the array of pointers can be addresses of variables or addresses of array elements or any other addresses.

Example

```
#include<stdio.h>
main()
{
```

```
        int *arr[4];
        int i=3,j=5,k=7,m=9,n;
        arr[0]=&i;
        arr[1]=&j;
        arr[2]=&k;
        arr[3]=&m;
        for(n=0;n<=3;n++)
        {
                printf(%d",(arr[n]));
        }
}
```

5.4 POINTERS TO FUNCTIONS

A useful technique is the ability to have pointers to functions. Their declaration is easy: write the declaration as it would be for the function, say

```
int func(int a, float b);
```

and simply put brackets around the name and a * in front of it: that declares the pointer. Because of precedence, if you don't parenthesize the name, you declare a function returning a pointer:

```
/* function returning pointer to int */
int *func(int a, float b);
/* pointer to function returning int */
int (*func)(int a, float b);
```

Once you've got the pointer, you can assign the address of the right sort of function just by using its name: like an array, a function name is turned into an address when it's used in an expression. You can call the function using one of two forms:

```
(*func)(1,2);
/* or */
func(1,2);
```

The second form has been newly blessed by the Standard. Here's a simple example.

```
#include <stdio.h>
#include <stdlib.h>
void func(int);
main(){
   void (*fp)(int);
   fp = func;
   (*fp)(1);
   fp(2);
   exit(EXIT_SUCCESS);
}
Void func(int arg){
   printf("%d\n", arg);
}
```

5.5 POINTERS AND ARRAYS

Pointers and arrays are very closely linked in C. Consider the following:

```
int a[10], x;
int *pa;
pa = &a[0]; /* pa pointer to address of a[0] */
x = *pa;
/* x = contents of pa (a[0] in this case) */
```

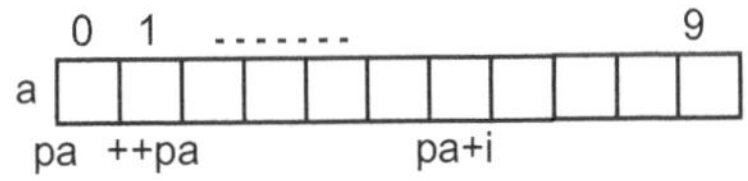

Figure 5.1: Arrays and Pointers

To get somewhere in the array (Fig.) using a pointer we could do:

$$pa + i \equiv a[i]$$

NOTE There is no bound checking of arrays and pointers so you can easily go beyond array memory and overwrite other things.

C however is much more subtle in its link between arrays and pointers.

For example we can just type

pa = a;

instead of pa = &a[0]

and a[i] can be written as *(a + i). *i.e.* &a[i] ≡ a + i.

We also express pointer addressing like this: pa[i] ≡ *(pa + i).

Example

```
#include<stdio.h>
main{}
{
        int *p,sum,I;
        Static int x[5]={5,9,6,3,7};
        i=0;
        p=x;
        printf("Element value address");
        while(i<5)
        {
                printf(x{%d]%d%u",I,*p,p);
                Sum=sum+*p;
                I++;p++;
        }
        prinf("sum=%d",sum);
        prinf(&x[0]=%u",&x[0]);
        printf("p=%u",p);
}
```

5.6 POINTERS AND STRUCTURES

These are fairly straight forward and are easily defined. Consider the following:

```
struct COORD {float x,y,z;} pt;
    struct COORD *pt_ptr;
pt_ptr = &pt; /* assigns pointer to pt */
```

the ->operator lets us access a member of the structure pointed to by a pointer. *i.e.*:

```
pt_ptr->x = 1.0;
pt_ptr->y = pt_ptr->y - 3.0;
```

Example: Linked Lists

```
typedef struct
{
        int value;
        ELEMENT *next;
} ELEMENT;
ELEMENT n1, n2;
n1.next = &n2;
```

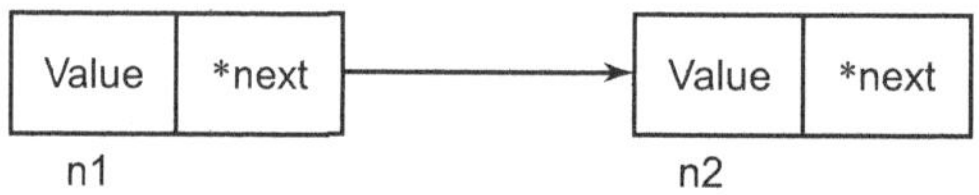

Figure 5.2: Linking Two Nodes

NOTE We can only declare next as a pointer to ELEMENT. We cannot have a element of the variable type as this would set up a *recursive* definition which is not allowed. We are allowed to set a pointer reference since 4 bytes are set aside for any pointer.

5.7 POINTERS AND FUNCTION

In a function declaration, the pointer are very much used. Sometimes, only with a pointer a complex function can be easily represented and success. In a function definition, the usage of the pointers may be classified into two groups:

1. Call by reference
2. Call by value.

5.7.1 Call by Value

We have seen that there will be a link established between the formal and actual parameters when a function is invoked. As soon as temporary storage is created where the value of actual parameters is stored. The formal parameters picks up its value from storage area the mechanism of data transfer between formal and actual parameters allows the actual parameters mechanism of data transfer is referred as call by value. The corresponding formal parameter always represents a local variable in the called function. The current value of the corresponding actual parameter becomes the initial value of formal parameter. In the body of the actual parameter, the value of formal parameter may be changed. In the body of the subprogram, the value of formal parameter may be changed by assignment or input statements. This will not change the value of the actual parameters.

Example

```
#include< stdio.h >
void main()
{
int x,y;
x=20;
y=30;
printf("\n Value of a and b before function call =%d %d",a,b);
fncn(x,y);
printf("\n Value of a and b after function call =%d %d",a,b);
}
fncn(p,q)
int p,q;
{
p=p+p;
q=q+q;
}
```

5.7.2 Call by Reference

The address should be pointers, when we pass address to a function the parameters receiving. By using pointers, the process of calling a function to pass the address of the variable is known as call by reference. The function which is called by reference can change the value of the variable used in the call.

Example

```
#include< stdio.h >
void main()
{
int x,y;
x=20;
y=30;
printf("\n Value of a and b before function call =%d %d",a,b);
fncn(&x,&y); printf("\n Value of a and b after function call =%d
%d",a,b);
}
fncn(p,q)
int p,q;
{
*p=*p+*p;
*q=*q+*q;
}
```

5.8 DYNAMIC MEMORY ALLOCATION

Dynamic allocation is a pretty unique feature to C. It enables us to create data types and structures of any size and length to suit our programs need within the program.

We will look at two common applications of this:

- Dynamic arrays
- Dynamic data structure e.g. linked lists

Malloc, Sizeof, and Free

The Function malloc is most commonly used to attempt to ``grab'' a continuous portion of memory. It is defined by:

```
void *malloc(size_t number_of_bytes)
```

That is to say it returns a pointer of type void * that is the start in memory of the reserved portion of size number_of_bytes. If memory cannot be allocated a NULL pointer is returned.

Since a void * is returned the C standard states that this pointer can be converted to any type. The size_t argument type is defined in stdlib.h and is an unsigned type.

```
char *cp;
cp = malloc(100);
```

Attempts to get 100 bytes and assigns the start address to cp.

Also it is usual to use the sizeof() function to specify the number of bytes:

```
int *ip;
ip = (int *) malloc(100*sizeof(int));
```

Some C compilers may require to cast the type of conversion. The (int *) means coercion to an integer pointer. Coercion to the correct pointer type is very important to ensure pointer arithmetic is performed correctly. I personally use it as a means of ensuring that I am totally correct in my coding and use cast all the time.

It is good practice to use size of () even if you know the actual size you want -- it makes for device independent (portable) code.

Sizeof can be used to find the size of any data type, variable or structure. Simply supply one of these as an argument to the function.

```
int i;
struct COORD {float x,y,z};
typedef struct COORD PT;
sizeof(int), sizeof(i),
sizeof(struct COORD) and
sizeof(PT) are all ACCEPTABLE
```

In the above we can use the link between pointers and arrays to treat the reserved memory like an array. *i.e* we can do things like:

```
ip[0] = 100;
```

or

```
for(i=0;i<100;++i) scanf("%d",ip++);
```

When you have finished using a portion of memory you should always free() it. This allows the memory *freed* to be available again, possibly for further malloc() calls.

The function free() takes a pointer as an argument and frees the memory to which the pointer refers.

5.9 COMMAND LINE INPUT OR ARGUMENTS

C lets read arguments from the command line which can then be used in our programs.

We can type arguments after the program name when we run the program.

In order to be able to use such arguments in our code we must define them as follows:

main(int argc, char **argv)

So our main function now has its own arguments. These are the only arguments main accepts.

- **argc** is the number of arguments typed -- including the program name.
- **argv** is an array of strings holding each command line argument -- including the program name in the first array element.

Example

```
#include<stdio.h>
main (int argc, char **argv)
{ /* program to print arguments from command line */
    int i;
    printf(``argc = %d'',argc);
    for (i=0;i<argc;++i)
    printf(``argv[%d]: %s\n'',i, argv[i]);
    }
```

Assume it is compiled to run it as args.

So if we type:

```
args f1 ``f2'' f3 4 stop!
```

The output would be:

```
argc = 6
argv[0] = args
argv[1] = f1
argv[2] = f2
argv[3] = f3
argv[4] = 4
argv[5] = stop!
```

5.10 FILES

A file is a collection of bytes stored on a secondary storage device, which is generally a disk of some kind. The collection of bytes may be interpreted, for example, as characters, words, lines, paragraphs and pages from a textual document; fields and records belonging to a database; or pixels from a graphical image. The meaning attached to a particular file is determined entirely by the data structures and operations used by a program to process the file. It is conceivable (and it sometimes happens) that a graphics file will be read and displayed by a program designed to process textual data.

File is a collection of records. The basic data file operations are naming, opening, reading, writing, and closing.

5.10.1 Creating a File

Creat( ) function is used to create a new file or to rewrite old files. The general form is

Int creat("filename",mode);

Where,

Int	- return type
Creat	- function name
Filename	- name of the file
Mode	- octal control digit to specify the access rights of a File

Example

```
Int fc;
Fc=create("muc",0754");
```

5.10.2 Reading a File

Reading a file means reading data from the opened or created file in read or read/write mode. The general format is

Int read(fc,buf,n);

Where,

Int	- return type
Read	- function name
Fc	- name of the already created file
Buf	- name of temporary memory area
N	- size of the data to read in terms of byte.

Example

```
Char buf[100];
Int I,fc;
Fc=open("muc",0);
I=read(fc,buf,100);
```

5.10.3 Writing a File

Writing a file means, writing data to a file opened or created in write or read/write mode. The general format is

In write(fc,nuf,n);

Example

Char buf[100];

Int I,fc;

Fc=open("muc",1);

I=write(fc,buf,100);

5.10.4 Opening a File

A file should be opened before reading from it or writing onto it. The fopen( ) function is used to open a stream or data file. If the file open operation is a success. The general format is

fopen("fileopen",mode);

The fopen function requires two arguments of type string. The first argument refers to the name of the file to be opened. The second refers to the mode, which specifies the purpose for which the file is opened.

Example

```
#include <stdio.h>
int main()
{
        char filename[80];
        FILE *fp;
        printf("File to be opened? ");
        scanf("%79s", filename);
        fp = fopen(filename,"r");
if (fp == NULL)
{
        fprintf(stderr, "Unable to open file
        %s\n", filename);
        return 1; /* Exit to operating system */
}
return 0;
}
```

5.10.5 Closing a File

A file is closed when all the input/output operations are complemented close a file which has been opened for use. The general format is

```
int fclose(file,*fp);
```

Example

```
---------------
---------------
file *p1,*p2;
P1=fopen("muc.txt","r");
```

```
P2=fopen("sal.txt","w");
---------------
--------------
fclose(p1);
fclose(p2);
```

5.11 OPERATIONS ON FILES

getc() and putc() functions are used to read or output a character similar to getchar and putchar functions. getchar reads character from the standard input unit. Putchar displays character from standard output unit. But getc is used to read a character form a file and putc routine is used to write a character into a file.

Example

Write a C program to open the file for reading.

```
#include<stdio.h>
main()
{
    file *fp;
    char a[50];
    fp=fopen("muc.txt","r");
    if(fp==NULL)
    {
            puts("Cannot open a file");
            exit();
    }
    while(fgets(s,79,fp)!=NULL)
    printf("%s",s);
    fclose(fp);
}
```

LET US SUMMARISE

- A pointer is a variable which contains the address in memory of another variable.
- To get the address of memory location allocated to a variable address operator(&) can be used.
- The address of a variable can be stored in another variable called the pointer variable.
- After assigning the address of a variable to a pointer variable that variable value can be accessed the pointer variable using the unary operator.
- C provides two special pointer operators to manipulate the data items directly form the memory location.

REVIEW QUESTIONS

1. Define Pointer.
2. How declaring a pointer?

3. What is indirect operator?
4. What is & operator?
5. List the operation on pointers.

EXERCISES

1. Write a C program to display the address of the variable.
2. Write a C program to print element and its address using pointer.
3. Write a C program to add two numbers through variables and their pointers.
4. Write a C program to write data to text file and read it.

APPNEDIX I

THIRUVALLUVAR UNIVERSITY (PRACTICAL EXERCISES)

1. Summation of Series: Sin(x) (Compare with built in functions)

```
/* Sine Series*/
#include<stdio.h>
#include<conio.h>
main()
{
float x,sum,term,y;
int n,i;
clrscr();
printf("\n Enter the value of x=");
scanf("%f",&x);
y=x;
printf("\n Enter the no of terms=");
scanf("%d",&n);
x=(x*3.1412)/180.0;
sum=x; term=x;
for(i=1;i<=n;i++)
{
term=(term*(-1)*x*x)/((2*i)*(2*i+1));
sum=sum+term;
}
printf("\n The sine series for x=%f =%10.6f",y,sum);
getch();
}
OUTPUT
-------------
```

```
Enter the value of x=30
Enter the no of terms=2
The sine series for x=30.00000 = 0.499945
```

2. **Summation of Series Cos(x) (Compare with built in functions)**

```
/*Cosine  Series */
#include<stdio.h>
#include<conio.h>
main()
{
 float x,sum=1,term=1,y;
 int n,i;
clrscr();
 printf("\n Enter the value of x=");
 scanf("%f",&x);
 y=x;
 printf("\n Enter the no of terms=");
 scanf("%d",&n);
 x=(x*3.1412)/180.0;
 for(i=1;i<=n;i++)
 {
  term=(term*(-1)*x*x)/((2*i)*(2*i-1));
  sum=sum+term;
 }
 printf("\n The cos series for x=%f = %10.6f",y,sum);
 getch();
}
OUTPUT
-------------
Enter the value of x=30
Enter the no of terms=2
The cos series for x=30.000000 = 0.866087
```

3. **Counting the no. of vowels, consonants, words, white spaces in a line of text and array of lines**

```
/* Counting vowels of given text * /
#include<stdio.h>
#include<conio.h>
main()
{
   char s[50];
   int i,c=0,w=1,v=0,len;
```

```
  clrscr();
  printf("\nEnter the text: ");
  gets(s);
  len=strlen(s);
  for(i=0;i<len;i++)
  {
   switch(toupper(s[i]))
   {
     case 'A':
     case 'E':
     case 'I':
     case 'O':
     case 'U': v++; break;
     case ' ': w++; break;
     default : c++; break;
   }
  }
     printf("\nThe given text: %s",s);
     printf("\nThe no. of vowels: %d",v);
     printf("\nThe no. of consonant: %d",c);
     printf("\nThe no. of words: %d",w);
     printf("\nThe no. of spaces: %d",w-1);
     getch();
 }
```

```
OUTPUT
-------------
Enter the text: shiek shafi
The given text: shiek shafi
The no. of vowels: 4
The no. of consonant: 6
The no. of words: 2
The no. of spaces: 1
```

4. Reverse a string & check for palindrome.

```
/*Checking Palindrome of given string*/
#include<stdio.h>
#include<conio.h>
#include<string.h>
main()
{
```

```
 int i,j,flag;
 char *s;
 clrscr();
 printf("\nEnter a string: ");
 gets(s);
 i=0;
 j=strlen(s);
 j=j-1;
 while(i<j&&flag)
 {
  if(s[i]!=s[j])
  flag=0;
  i++;
  j--;
 }
 printf("\nThe given string is: %s",s);
 flag?printf("\nPalindrome"):printf("\nNot Palindrome");
 getch();
}
OUTPUT
-------------
Enter the string: liril
The given string is: liril
Palindrome
Enter the string: hamam
The given string is: hamam
Not Palindrome
```

5. **nPr, nCr in a single program.**

```
#include <stdio.h>
#include <conio.h>
long double fact( int p)
{
long double prod = 1;
int i;
for( i = 1; i<= p; i++) // multiply 'i' with prod where 'i' varies
from 1 to n
prod = prod * i;
return( prod); // n! factorial is returned
}
int ncr ( int n, int r)
```

```
{
return( fact( n) / (fact( r) * fact(n- r) ) ) ; // return ncr results
}
long npr( int n , int r)
{
return( fact( n) / fact( n- r)); // return npr result
}
main()
{
int n , r, ncr( int , int);
long npr( int , int);
long double fact( int);
printf(" enter value of n & r \n");
scanf("%d %d",&n , &r);
if( n>= r) // test user entered inputs are valid or not
{
printf( " ncr is %d\n", ncr( n , r)); // display results of ncr and npr
printf(" npr is %ld", npr( n, r));
}
else
printf(" n cannot be less than r");
getch();
}
```

6. **GCD of two Numbers**

```
/*Finding GCD of two values*/
#include<stdio.h>
#include<conio.h>
main()
{
 int a,b,gcd,t1,t2;
 clrscr();
 printf("\nEnter two values:\n");
 scanf("%d%d",&a,&b);
 t1=a; t2=b;
 gcd=mygcd(a,b);
 printf("\nGiven values are: a=%d, b=%d",t1,t2);
 printf("\n\nGCD = %d",gcd);
 getch();
}
```

```
int mygcd(int a,int b)
{ int r;
  r=a%b;
  if(r==0)
  return b;
  else
  mygcd(b,r);
}
```

```
OUTPUT
------------
Enter two values:
15
25
Given values are: a=15, b=25
GCD = 5
```

7. Bubble Sort

```
/*Bubble Sort*/
#include<stdio.h>
#include<conio.h>
main()
{   int a[]={10,25,5,70,45};
    int n=5,i,j,temp;
    clrscr();
    printf("\n       BUBBLE SORT");
    printf("\nThe given values are:");
    for(i=0;i<n;i++)
    printf("%5d",a[i]);
    for(i=0;i<n-1;i++)
    for(j=0;j<n-1;j++)
    if(a[j] > a[j+1])
    { temp=a[j];
      a[j]=a[j+1];
      a[j+1]=temp;
    }
    printf("\nThe sorted numbers are:");
    for(i=0;i<n;i++)
    printf("%5d",a[i]);
    getch();
}
```

```
OUTPUT
--------------
BUBBLE SORT
The given values are: 10 25 5 70 45
The sorted numbers are:5 10 25 45 70
```

8. Linear Search

```
/* Linear Search*/
    #include<stdio.h>
    #include<conio.h>
    main()
    {
      int a[]={12,27,5,83,94,36,72,11,54,43};
      int i=0,n=10,x,found=0;
      clrscr();
      printf("\n Enter a Number to search : ");
      scanf("%d",&x);
      while(i<n&&!found)
      if(a[i++]==x)
      found=1;
      found?
      printf("\t%d : is found",x):printf("\t%d: not found",x);
      getch();
    }
OUTPUT
-------------
Enter a Number to search :
94
94 : is found
Enter a Number to search :
100
100 : is not found.
```

9. Demonstration of pointer arithmetic.

/* a program to display the memory address of a variable using pointer and to add with an integer quantity with pointer and to display the content of the pointer */

```
#include<stdio.h>
main()
{
int x;
int *ptr1,*ptr2;
x=10;
```

```
ptr1=&x;
ptr2=ptr1+6;
printf("value of x=%d\n",x);
printf("content of ptr1=%d\n",*ptr1);
printf("address of ptr1=%u\n",ptr1);
printf("adress of ptr2=(ptr+6)=%u\n",ptr2);
printf("contents of ptr2=%d\n",*ptr2);
}
/* end */
OUTPUT
-------------
value of x=10
content of ptr1=10
address of ptr1=65496
adress of ptr2=(ptr+6)=65508
contents of ptr2=-24
```

10. Find the maximum and minimum number of a set

```
#include<stdio.h>
main()
{
int a[50],max,min,n;
printf("enter the noof digits\n");
scanf("%d",&n);
printf("\nenter the numbers");
for(i=0;i<n;i++)
{
scanf("%d",&a[i]);
}
max=a[0];
min=a[0];
for(i=1;i<n;i++)
{
if(max<a[i])
max=a[i];
if(min>a[i])
min=a[i];
}
printf("\n max is %d \n min is %d",max ,min);
}
```

11. Merge two arrays of integers both with their elements in ascending order into a single ordered array.

```
/* Program to merge two sorted arrays */
#include<stdio.h>
int merge(int[],int[],int[],int,int);
main()
{
int a[20],b[20],c[40],n,m,i,p;
printf("\nEnter the no.of element present in the first array: ");
scanf("%d",&n);
printf("\nEnter the first array.......\n");
for(i=0;i<n;i++)
scanf("%d",&a[i]);
printf("\nEnter the no. of element present in the second array: ");
scanf("%d",&m);
printf("\nEnter the second array.......\n");
for(i=0;i<m;i++)
scanf("%d",&b[i]);
p=merge(a,b,c,n,m);
printf("\nThe merged array is.........\n");
for(i=0;i<p;i++)
printf("%d  ",c[i]);
printf("\n\n");
}
int merge(int a[],int b[],int c[],int n,int m)
{
int i=0,j=0,k=0;
while(i<n&&j<m)
{
if(a[i]<b[j])
{
c[k]=a[i];
i++; k++;
}
else if(a[i]>b[j])
{
c[k]=b[j];
j++;   k++;
}
else                    // to avoid duplication
```

```
{
 c[k]=a[i];
 i++;  j++;  k++;
 }
 }
 for(;i<n;i++,k++)
 c[k]=a[i];
 for(;j<m;j++,k++)
 c[k]=b[j];
 return k;
 }
```

APPNEDIX II

PERIYAR UNIVERSITY (PRACTICAL EXERCISES)

1. **Write a program to find the largest number and smaller number by using if statement**

```
#include<stdio.h>
main()
{
int c1,c2,c3;
printf("enter values of c1,c2,and c3");
scanf("%d%d%d",&c1,&c2,&c3);
if((c1<c2)&&(c1<c3))
printf("\n c1 is less than c2 and c3");
if(!(c1<c2))
printf("\n c1 is greater than c2");
if((c1<c2)||(c1<c3))
printf("\n c1 is less than c2 or c3 or both");
}
```

2. **Write a program to convert the decimal to binary conversion by using while statement**

```
#include <stdio.h>
#include <math.h>
int getBinary(int);
int main(void)
{
   int integer;
   printf("Enter decimal [base 10] integer: ");
   scanf("%d", &integer);
  getBinary(integer);
   return(0);
}
```

```
int getBinary(int integer)
{
  int remainder;
  while (integer > 0)
    {
     remainder = integer % 2;
     printf("%d", remainder);
     integer = integer / 2;
    }
  printf("\n");
  return(integer);
}
```

3. **Write a program to count the positive, negative & zero numbers.**

```
#include<stdio.h>
#include<conio.h>
#define size 15
void main()
{
int input[size],i,neg=0,pos=0,zro=0;
clrscr();
printf("how many elements you want enter(should be less than %d:",size);
scanf("%d",&n);
printf(«enter elements into array:\n»);
for(i=0;i<n;i++)
scanf(«%d»,&input[i]);
for(i=0;i<n;i++)
{
if(input[i]>0)
pos++;
if(input[i]<0)
neg++;
if(input[i]==0)
zro++;
}
printf(«number of positive elements:%d\n»,pos);
printf(«number of negetive elements:%d\n»,neg);
printf(«number of zero elements:%d\n»,zro);
getch();
}
```

4. **Write a program to check whether a given number is a prime or not.**

```
include<stdio.h>
int main(){
     int num,i,count=0;
     printf("Enter a number: ");
     scanf("%d",&num);
     for(i=2;i<=num/2;i++){
          if(num%i==0){
           count++;
               break;
          }
     }
    if(count==0 && num!= 1)
          printf("%d is a prime number",num);
    else
       printf("%d is not a prime number",num);
    return 0;
}
```

5. **Write a program to display the Fibonacci series.**

```
#include<stdio.h>
int main(){
     int k,r;
     long int i=0l,j=1,f;
     //Taking maximum numbers form user
     printf("Enter the number range:");
     scanf("%d",&r);
     printf("FIBONACCI SERIES: ");
     printf("%ld %ld",i,j); //printing firts two values.
     for(k=2;k<r;k++){
           f=i+j;
           i=j;
           j=f;
           printf(" %ld",j);
     }
       return 0;
}
```

6. **Write a program to concatenate two strings without using string library function.**

```
#include<stdio.h>
#include<conio.h>
```

```
void main()
{
char a[10],b[10],c[40];
int i,j;
clrscr();
printf("\n\nENTER FIRST STRING:");
gets(a);
printf("\n\nENTER SECOND STRING:");
gets(b);
for(i=0;a[i]!='\0';i++)
c[i]=a[i];
for(j=0;a[j]!='\0';j++)
{
c[i]=b[j];
i++;
}
c[i]='\0';
printf("\n\nTHE COMBINED STRING IS:");
puts(c);
getch();
}
```

7. **Write a program to count the number of vowels, consonants, and digits in a line of Text.**

```
#include<stdio.h>
#include<conio.h>
main()
{
   char s[50];
   int i,c=0,w=1,v=0,len;
   clrscr();
   printf("\nEnter the text: ");
   gets(s);
   len=strlen(s);
   for(i=0;i<len;i++)
   {
    switch(toupper(s[i]))
    {
      case 'A':
      case 'E':
      case 'I':
```

```
        case 'O':
        case 'U': v++; break;
        case ' ': w++; break;
        default : c++; break;
      }
    }
        printf("\nThe given text: %s",s);
        printf("\nThe no. of vowels: %d",v);
        printf("\nThe no. of consonant: %d",c);
        printf("\nThe no. of words: %d",w);
        printf("\nThe no. of spaces: %d",w-1);
        getch();
   }
```

8. **Write a program to reverse a String.**

```
#include<stdio.h>
#include<conio.h>
void main()
{
int i=0;
char str[10];
clrscr();
printf("Enter the string:");
scanf("%c",str);
while(str[i]!='\0')
i++;
for(i=0;str[i]!='\0';i++)
{
str1[j]=str[i];
j++;
}
str1[j]='\0';
printf("Reverse of a given string:",str1);
getch();
}
```

9. **Write a program to design the calculator functions as (i) Addition (ii) Subtraction & (iii) Multiplication function.**

```
#include<stdio.h>
/*Function for Addition*/
add(int a,int b)
{
```

```
clrscr();
c=a+b;
return(c);
}
/*Function for Subtraction*/
sub(int a,int b);
{
clrscr();
c=a-b;
return(c);
}
/*Function for Multiplication*/
mul(int a,int b)
{
clrscr();
c=a*b;
return(c);
}
/*Function Main*/
main()
{
int choice,n1,n2,ans;
clrscr();
printf("Please Choose : \n");
printf("1.Addition\n2.Subtraction\n3.Multiplication");
scanf("%d",choice);
printf("\nPlease enter First Number for Calculation : ");
scanf("%d",n1);
printf("\nEnter the Second Number for Calculation : ");
if(choice==1)
{
ans=add(n1,n2);
printf("The Answer is :%d",ans);
}
else if(choice==2)
{
ans=sub(n1,n2);
printf("The Answer is :%d",ans);
}
```

```
else if(choice==3)
{
ans=mul(n1,n2);
printf("The Answer is :%d",ans);
}
/*If all these are not selected*/
else
{
printf("Out Of Range");
}
getch();
}
```

10. Write a program to find the factorial of a number using recursion.

```
#include<stdio.h>
int fact(int);
int main(){
   int num,f;
   printf("\nEnter a number: ");
   scanf("%d",&num);
   f=fact(num);
   printf("\nFactorial of %d is: %d",num,f);
   return 0;
}
int fact(int n){
    if(n==1)
         return 1;
    else
         return(n*fact(n-1));
 }
```

11. Write a program for ascending order of given N Numbers.

```
#include<stdio.h>
#include<conio.h>
void main()
{
int i,arr[20],num,min,temp,j;
clrscr();
printf("\nEnter the num's of element to sorted in ascending order ");
scanf("%d",&num);
printf("enter %d num's",num);
```

```
for(i=0;i<num;i++)
{
scanf("%d",&arr[i]);
}
 printf("\nur orignal list\n");
for(i=0;i<num;i++)
{
  printf(" %d",arr[i]);
}
 for(i=0;i<num;i++)
{
  min=i;
  for(j=i+1;j<num;j++)
  {
   if(arr[min]>arr[j])
    min=j;
  }
  if(min!=i)
  {
   temp=arr[i];
   arr[i]=arr[min];
   arr[min]=temp;
  }
 }
 printf("\nur sorted list\n");
 for(i=0;i<num;i++)
 {
  printf(" %d",arr[i]);
 }
getch();
}
```

12. **Write a program to separate odd and even numbers using file.**

```
#include<stdio.h>
#include<math.h>
void main()
{
FILE *all,*even,*odd;
int number,i,records;
printf("input the total number of records that u want to enter");
scanf("%d",& records);
```

```
all=fopen("ANYNUMBER","w");
for(i=1;i<=records;i++)
{
scanf("%d",&number);
if(number==-1)break;
putw(number,all);
}
fclose(all);
all=fopen("ANYNUMBER","r");
even=fopen("EVENNUMBER","w");
odd=fopen("ODDNUMBER","w");
while((number=getw(all))!=EOF)
{
if(number%2==0)
putw(number,even);
else
putw(number,odd);
}
fclose(all);
fclose(even);
fclose(odd);
even=fopen("EVENNUMBER","r");
odd=fopen("ODDNUMBER","r");
printf(" THE EVEN NUMBERS ARE");
while((number=getw(even))!=EOF)
printf(" %4d",number);
printf(" THE ODD NUMBERS ARE");
while((number=getw(odd))!=EOF)
printf("  %4d",number);
fclose(even);
fclose(odd);
}
```

INDEX